2022
Feng Shui Planner & Calendar

Year of the Tiger

壬寅

PictureHealer | Shih-Tien Wu

To learn more about Feng Shui and Chinese fortune-telling, please visit **www.PictureHealer.com** and subscribe to our **YouTube channel: PictureHealer** for weekly videos.

Sign up for our email list for the latest updates and free downloads.

https://sendfox.com/picturehealer

Table of contents

All about 2022, the year of the Tiger

The starting date for the 2022 Tiger year

The lunar new year of 2022 is on February 1st. For the fortune-telling and Feng Shui purpose, the starting of the Tiger year is based on **Li Chun (立春, start of spring)**, one of the 24 solar terms. This year, it falls on **February 4th.** People born before February 04 still belong to the Ox sign, and **the Tiger year starts from February 04, 2022, to February 04, 2023.** In general, we still call 2022 a Tiger year.

"Ren Yin" (壬寅) year and the Water Tiger

Based on the Chinese 10 Heavenly stems and 12 Earthly branches timing system, **2022 is the year of Ren Yin (壬寅).** It has the energy of **water, wood, and metal** according to the 5-element theory and the Na Yin system. 2022 is a **Water Tiger** year.

Since we are still in Feng Shui period 8 (2004-2023), the Earth element of star 8 is still strong and lucky.
We have water, wood, metal, and earth this year. These element-related careers and characters will be highlighted in 2022. The only element missing is the fire. Overall, this is a balanced year.

10 Heavenly Stems

1. **Jia** Yang Wood
2. **Yi** Yin Wood
3. **Bing** Yang Fire
4. **Ding** Yin Fire
5. **Wu** Yang Earth
6. **Ji** Yin Earth
7. **Geng** Yang Metal
8. **Xin** Yin Metal
9. **Ren** Yang Water
10. **Kui** Yin Water

12 Earthly Branches

1. **Zi** Rat Yang Water
2. **Chou** Ox Yin Earth
3. **Yin** Tiger Yang Wood
4. **Mao** Rabbit Yin Wood
5. **Chen** Dragoon Yang Earth
6. **Si** Snake Yin Fire
7. **Wu** Horse Yang Fire
8. **Wei** Goat Yin Earth
9. **Shen** Monkey Yang Metal
10. **You** Rooster Yin Metal
11. **Xu** Dog Yang Earth
12. **Hai** Pig Yin Water

The 10 Heavenly Stems and 12 Earthly Branches creates 60 combinations.

2022 prediction from old poems

There are poems written in ancient times predicting each year. Here is our interpretation of the 2022 tiger year prediction based on **the Yellow Emperor Earth Mother (Di Mu) classics.**

"There is an abundance of grains and crops, and enough rain in all 4 seasons. Silk production from mulberry leaves becomes expensive. Farmers and ordinary people are joyful about the peace and harvest of the year. Animals can be affected by a pandemic but proper prevention can stop the spread."

There is enough production in farming and food this year, but the price can go very high for daily necessities. There could be inflation making standard of living harder to be maintained. Watch out for diseases affecting animals. Pay attention to prevent any spread of diseases.

The East and West will be luckier than North in 2022

In a very simplified way, we can say East and West are lucky directions this year. Luck usually alternates between the East-West and the North-South each year. **The general unlucky direction is the North in 2022. Try to avoid construction in the North this year.**

For more detailed lucky and unlucky directions, we will look at the yearly Flying Star Feng Shui chart next.

2022 Tai Sui (Grand Duke Jupiter)

Tai Sui is the governing god of the year. It is based on historical figures of military leaders. There are 60 Tai Sui gods based on the 60 combinations of the old stem-branches timing system. In the 2022 year of the Tiger, the name of the Tai Sui general is **"He Er" (賀諤)**.

Animal signs that clash with Tai Sui: Tiger and Monkey

The Tai Sui direction is the same as the animal sign of the year. **The Tiger direction is Northeast toward East on the 24 mountains (24 directions) in 2022.** See the chart below. In 2022, the most affected animal sign is the Tiger, and the second one is the Monkey, which is directly opposite the Tiger. **Both Tiger and Monkey signs are clashing with Tai Sui this year.**

It is believed that Tai Sui can bring **uncertainty and disruptions** to the affected animal signs. The general advice is to **stay conservative and avoid arguments, fighting, or any risky investments** during this year. However, this can also be a year of new opportunities and a major turning point in life. Instead of settling down with the old routine, you could be forced into new directions. Be flexible and be ready to adjust your plan quickly.

The old-fashioned way to "appease" Tai Sui is to pray at a temple or set up a Tai Sui altar at home with regular offerings. **"Pi Xiu"** is a powerful Feng Shui cure for people affected by Tai Sui. Display a Pi Xiu statue in the "Northeast toward East" of your house (Tiger direction), or carry a Pi Xiu key chain or Tai Shui card for protection. Doing good deeds and charity work can help your luck too.

Sui Po (Year Breaker) and San Sha (3-Killings) afflictions

Opposite to Tai Sui is the **Sui Po (Year Breaker)**. It is located at **Southwest toward West (SW3)** on the 24 directions. It is affecting the animal sign of **Monkey** this year.

San Sha or the 3-Killings include the whole North area this year. It could bring all kinds of problems such as health or financial issues. Try to avoid setting up important rooms here or doing construction in North this year.

It is better **not to face Tai Sui (NE3) when sitting down** on a chair or Sofa to avoid confronting Tai Sui god.

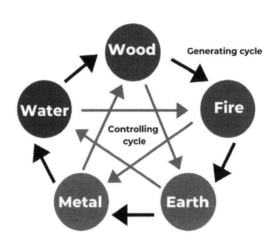

The Five-Element Cycle

Tai Sui, Sui Po, San Sha

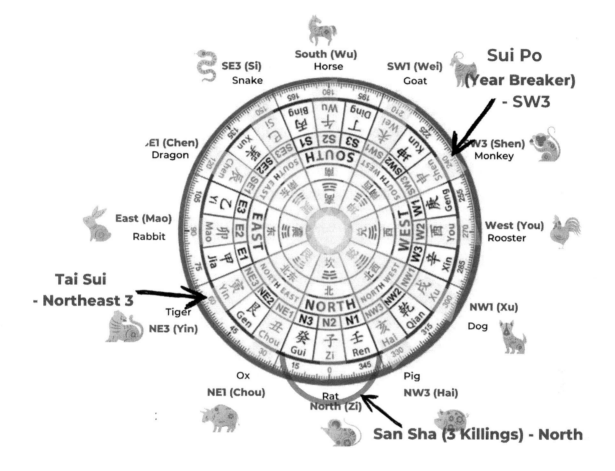

Avoid construction in the areas of Tai Sui, Sui Po, San Sha, and flying stars #2 (SW) and #5 (Center).

Flying Star Feng Shui

The Flying Star is a classical school of Feng Shui based on the 9 stars. The 9 stars fly to new sectors every year creating different energy. The yearly Flying Star Feng Shui chart is like an energy map. It helps us locate the lucky areas and set up rooms and furniture accordingly.

Below is the 2022 Flying Star Feng Shui chart. Notice the South is on the top. That is the traditional Chinese map format. Flip around to overlay on top of your floor plan so the North matches North.

	Southeast	South	Southwest	
	4 (Wood) Green — Intelligence, romance	**9** (Fire) Purple — Festivity, celebration	**2** (Earth) Black — Illness,	*Sui Po (Year breaker)* - Southwest toward West
East	**3** (Wood) Jade — Conflict, argument	**5** (Earth) Yellow — Obstacle, accident, illness	**7** (Metal) Red — Robbery, fighting	West
Tai Sui (yearly God) - Northeast toward East	**8** (Earth) White — Prosperity, good health	**1** (Water) White — Civil/scholarly career, fame, relationship	**6** (Metal) White — Physical/military career, power, Travel	
	Northeast	North	Northwest	

San Sha (3 Killings) - North

2022 Yearly Flying Star Feng Shui Chart

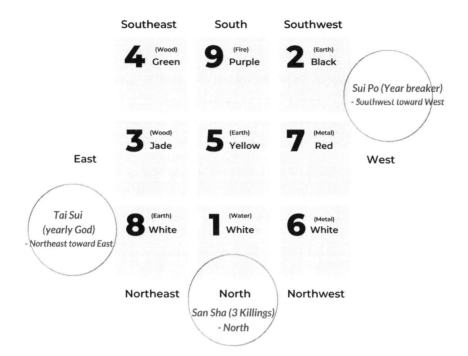

Southeast	South	Southwest
4 (Wood) Green	**9** (Fire) Purple	**2** (Earth) Black
3 (Wood) Jade	**5** (Earth) Yellow	**7** (Metal) Red
8 (Earth) White	**1** (Water) White	**6** (Metal) White

East

West

Sui Po (Year breaker)
- Southwest toward West

Tai Sui (yearly God)
- Northeast toward East

Northeast

North

Northwest

San Sha (3 Killings)
- North

1. To control Tai Sui, Sui Po, San Sha

In the Tai Sui direction (Northeast toward east), add:
- **Tai Sui card or amulet**

General Feng Shui cures for Tai Sui, Sui Po, and San Sha (Northeast, North, and Southwest):
- **Qi Lin**
- **Pi Xiu**
- **Dragon turtle**

*** Avoid facing Tai Sui direction when sitting down long term (eg. desk or sofa facing Northeast).

*** Avoid sitting in the San Sha direction (North) which faces South.

*** Avoid construction in these 3 areas.

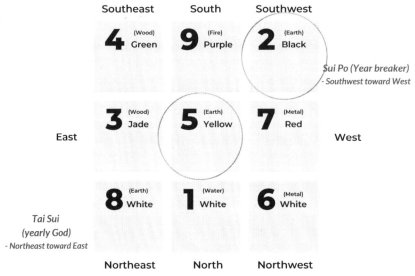

Southeast	South	Southwest
4 (Wood) Green	**9** (Fire) Purple	**2** (Earth) Black
		Sui Po (Year breaker) *- Southwest toward West*

East

| **3** (Wood) Jade | **5** (Earth) Yellow | **7** (Metal) Red |

West

Tai Sui *(yearly God)* *- Northeast toward East*

| **8** (Earth) White | **1** (Water) White | **6** (Metal) White |

| Northeast | North | Northwest |

San Sha (3 Killings) - North

2. To reduce illness, accidents, or obstacles (stars 2 and 5)

In the Center (5 Yellow) and Southwest (2 Black star):

Add metal objects such as:
- **Bronze bell,**
- **Bronze Hulu (gourd)**
- **6 Emperors' coins**

Or, add a **saltwater cure** (natural salt in a jar with an open lid to absorb negative energy).

Suitable colors:
- **Black, blue, or white/silver/gold.**
Avoid colors:
- **Red, purple.**

** Avoid construction in these areas.

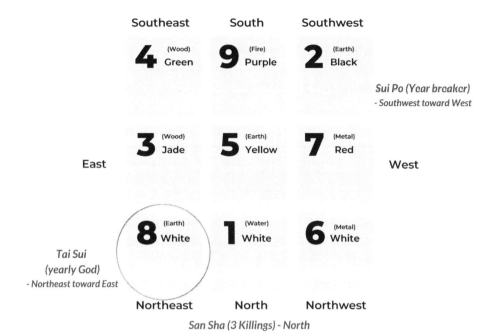

Southeast	**South**	**Southwest**
4 (Wood) Green	**9** (Fire) Purple	**2** (Earth) Black
East		*Sui Po (Year breaker)* - Southwest toward West
3 (Wood) Jade	**5** (Earth) Yellow	**7** (Metal) Red
		West
8 (Earth) White	**1** (Water) White	**6** (Metal) White
Tai Sui (yearly God) - Northeast toward East		
Northeast	**North**	**Northwest**

San Sha (3 Killings) - North

3. To enhance wealth luck (star 8)

In the Northeast (8 White star), add **any** Earth or Fire elements

- Ceramic or porcelain vase/teapot ✓
- Jade or crystal (Amethyst)
- Color or red, purple, yellow, or brown
- Any money enhancer (money jar, money frog, money god...)

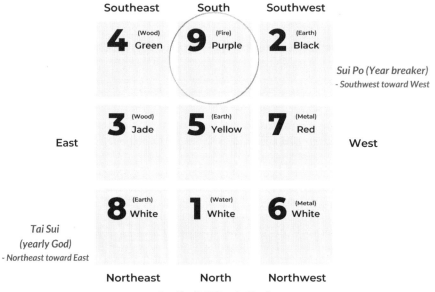

Southeast	South	Southwest
4 (Wood) Green	**9** (Fire) Purple	**2** (Earth) Black
3 (Wood) Jade	**5** (Earth) Yellow	**7** (Metal) Red
8 (Earth) White	**1** (Water) White	**6** (Metal) White
Northeast	North	Northwest

East

West

Sui Po (Year breaker)
- Southwest toward West

Tai Sui
(yearly God)
- Northeast toward East

San Sha (3 Killings) - North

4. To enhance festivity, romance, and relationship luck (star 9)

In the South (9 Purple star), add any Wood or Fire elements

- **Red candles or lanterns**
- **Red flowers**
- **Amethyst crystal**
- **Colors of red, purple, pink, or green**
- **Lucky bamboo**

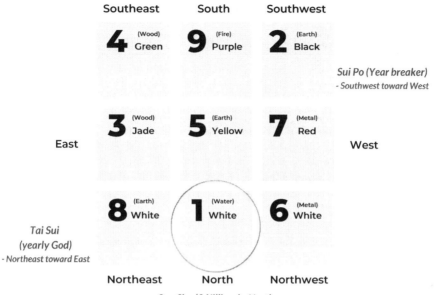

Southeast	South	Southwest
4 (Wood) Green	**9** (Fire) Purple	**2** (Earth) Black
3 (Wood) Jade	**5** (Earth) Yellow	**7** (Metal) Red
8 (Earth) White	**1** (Water) White	**6** (Metal) White

Sui Po (Year breaker)
- Southwest toward West

East

West

Tai Sui
(yearly God)
- Northeast toward East

Northeast   North   Northwest

San Sha (3 Killings) - North

5. To enhance (office/Civil type 文) career luck, romance, promotion (star 1 White)

In the North (1 White star), add

- **Wen Chang Pagoda**
- **Chinese ink brush set**
- **Painting of 9 Koi fishes**
- **Painting of dragons or horses**

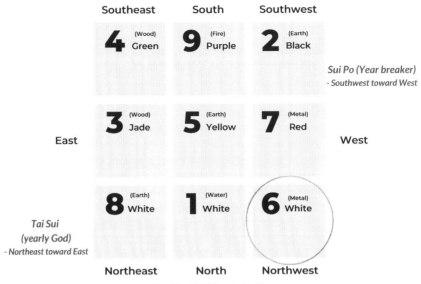

	Southeast	South	Southwest
	4 (Wood) Green	**9** (Fire) Purple	**2** (Earth) Black
East	**3** (Wood) Jade	**5** (Earth) Yellow	**7** (Metal) Red	West
	8 (Earth) White	**1** (Water) White	**6** (Metal) White
	Northeast	North	Northwest

Sui Po (Year breaker)
- Southwest toward West

Tai Sui
(yearly God)
- Northeast toward East

San Sha (3 Killings) - North

6. To enhance (physical/militarytype 武) career luck, power, travel (star 6 White)

In the Northwest (6 White star), add

- Bronze *Qi Lin*
- Bronze *dragon*
- Statue of a *horse* ✓
- Painting of *dragons or horses*
- Any t*rophy or award* ✓
- Add the color of *yellow/brown (*Earth)
- Avoid the color of *red/purple* (Fire)

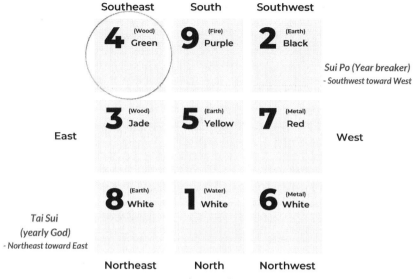

Southeast	South	Southwest
4 (Wood) Green	**9** (Fire) Purple	**2** (Earth) Black

Sui Po (Year breaker)
- Southwest toward West

East

3 (Wood) Jade	**5** (Earth) Yellow	**7** (Metal) Red

West

Tai Sui
(yearly God)
- Northeast toward East

8 (Earth) White	**1** (Water) White	**6** (Metal) White

| Northeast | North | Northwest |

San Sha (3 Killings) - North

7. To enhance intelligence, wisdom, romance, helpful people (star 4 Green)

In the Southeast (4 Green star), add

- Wen Chang Pagoda
- Chinese ink brush set ✓
- 4 lucky bamboos ✓
- Green plants
- Add Water elements such as the color of blue/black

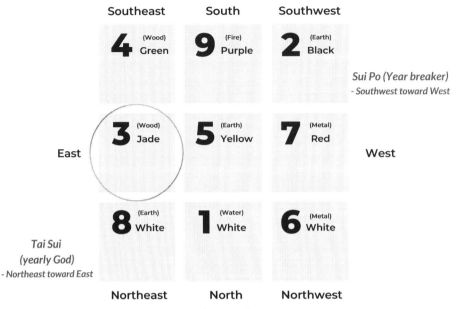

Southeast	South	Southwest
4 (Wood) Green	**9** (Fire) Purple	**2** (Earth) Black
3 (Wood) Jade	**5** (Earth) Yellow	**7** (Metal) Red
8 (Earth) White	**1** (Water) White	**6** (Metal) White

East — (circled 3 Jade)

West

Sui Po (Year breaker)
- Southwest toward West

Tai Sui
(yearly God)
- Northeast toward East

| Northeast | North | Northwest |

San Sha (3 Killings) - North

8. To control the conflict, argument, negative people, or legal issues (star 3 Jade)

In the East (3 Jade star), add Metal or Fire elements:

- Luo Pan (Feng Shui compass) or Ba Gua
- Bronze dragon turtle
- Bronze Qi Lin/Pi Xiu
- Add colors of red/purple (Fire) or white/silver (Metal).
- Avoid blue/black (Water) or green (Wood colors).

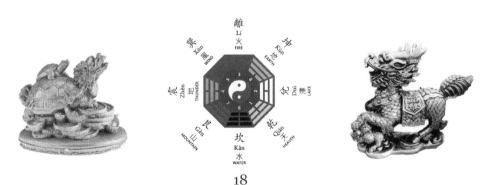

18

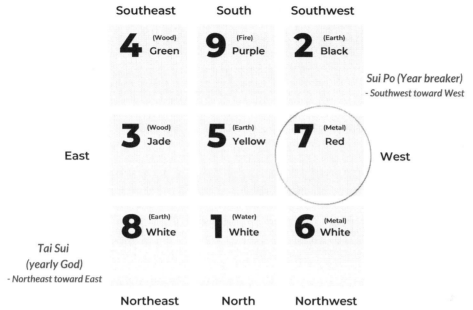

Southeast	**South**	**Southwest**
4 (Wood) Green	**9** (Fire) Purple	**2** (Earth) Black
East **3** (Wood) Jade	**5** (Earth) Yellow	**7** (Metal) Red **West**
8 (Earth) White	**1** (Water) White	**6** (Metal) White
Northeast	**North**	**Northwest**

Sui Po (Year breaker)
- Southwest toward West

Tai Sui
(yearly God)
- Northeast toward East

San Sha (3 Killings) - North

9. To control robbery, fighting, accidents, money loss, or legal trouble (7 Red star)

In the West (7 Red star), add Water element:

- Saltwater cure
- Picture or painting of water/ocean
- Add colors of black or blue (eg, black area rug)
- Avoid colors of yellow or brown (Earth)
- Luo Pan (feng shui compass) or Ba Gua
- Qi Lin or Pi Xiu

1. Rat in 2022

Born in 1936, 1948, 1960, 1972, 1984, 1996, 2008, 2020

More negative stars in the sign of Rat this year. Watch out for *illness, accident, and wrong investment causing money loss.*

It is better to focus on your own business and career. Combine your resources from different fields and people to create new opportunities.

Stay more conservative this year. Avoid impulsive fighting or quarrels. Safety and harmony are more important now.

Watch out for *petty people (Xiao Ren)* bringing trouble behind you.

3 lucky months:

Lunar April - helpful people (Gui Ren), peace, and harmony.
Lunar August - happy events, fame, and wealth.
Lunar December - career success, increased income, and happy relationship.

3 unlucky months:

Lunar February - conflict, fighting, or relationship trouble.
Lunar May - watch out for **travel safety** and **money loss.**
Lunar December - Illness, injury, or decreased wealth.

2. Ox in 2022

Born in 1937, 1949, 1961, 1973, 1985, 1997, 2009, 2021

There is a "wedding-luck" star in Ox this year. Ox can enjoy a happy love relationship and family life. This is a good year for a single Ox to get married.

There are helpful people (Gui Ren) in your sign this year. Expect career success and study luck.

There is an illness star in your sign this year. Exercise regularly and avoid overworking. Don't delay seeing a doctor.

Watch out for *petty people (Xiao Ren)* bringing trouble behind you. Avoid gossip or quarrel.

3 lucky months:

Lunar July - 2 lucky stars bring you **happiness and good wealth.**
Lunar August - the "3-harmony" star brings **helpful people and prosperity.**
Lunar November - the "6-harmony" star brings **increased luck in career and income.**

3 unlucky months:

Lunar March - illness, money wasted, or possible legal issues.
Lunar June- possible **accident, illness, or money loss.**
Lunar December - a star related to **injury or accidents.** Watch for travel safety.

牛

3. Tiger in 2022

Born in 1938, 1950, 1962, 1974, 1986, 1998, 2010, 2022

The "Wen Chang" star is in the sign of Tiger in 2022. It makes the Tigers extra smart this year. You can pass exams, come up with clever solutions, and write articles easily this year.

Tai Sui (yearly god) is in the sign of Tiger in 2022. It can bring unexpected up-and-downs. Stay conservative and do more charity work this year.

Together with the "Sword blade" star and other negative stars, there will be an increased chance of injury, quarrel, or legal trouble.

There will be obstacles and setbacks, but the outcome will be positive in the end.

3 lucky months:

Lunar May - increased wealth luck, happiness, and harmony.
Lunar August - 2 lucky stars bring fame, success, and prosperity.
Lunar October - the "6-harmony" star brings wealth, happiness, and helpful people.

3 unlucky months:

Lunar January - money loss, illness, or accidents.
Lunar July - watch out for accidents or money loss.
Lunar November - Avoid fighting, arguments, or petty people (Xiao Ren) causing trouble behind you.

4. Rabbit in 2022

Anara

Born in 1939, 1951, 1963, 1975, 1987, 1999, 2011,

The Tai Yang star (the Sun) is in the Rabbit sign in 2022. This star brings a harmonious relationship, helpful people, and wealth luck. It makes everything easier this year.

It is a lucky year for you in general. Don't forget to care for your close family and friends even if you are very busy.

There is also a peach blossom star for relationship or marriage luck. It can also bring relationship trouble if you are not careful.

Several negative stars can bring legal issues or trouble from petty people (Xiao Ren).

There is a "sky" star in the chart. Avoid travel to faraway countries this year.

3 lucky months:

Lunar March - Tai Yang star increases **wealth and prosperity.**
Lunar May - "Tian Xi" star increases **wealth luck and career promotion.**
Lunar July - Increased happiness and income.

3 unlucky months:

Lunar February - possible **accidents, injury, or money loss.**
Lunar August - **illness, gossip, and** watch out for **travel safety.**
Lunar September - illness, money loss, or legal issues.

5. Dragon in 2022

Born in 1928, 1940, 1952, 1964, 1976, 1988, 2000, 2012

Many negative stars (喪門, 地喪, 天哭, 月殺…) are in the sign of the dragon in 2022. They are related to **health issues, accidents, isolation, reduced wealth or wasting of your resources.**

Try to connect or team up with **lucky friends, coworkers, or family members** this year.

Avoid fighting or arguments Avoid risky investments **Stay conservative and take good care of your health.**

It is a good idea to do more charity work, **share what you have, and help other people in need.**

3 lucky months:

Lunar April - Lucky stars (天喜, 太陽) bring **happiness, prosperity, career success.**
Lunar August - The "6-harmony" (六合) star brings **good fortune.** The "Peach blossom" star (桃花) star can bring either **relationship luck or relationship trouble.**
Lunar December - Lucky star "Fu De" (福德) brings **prosperity and success.**

3 unlucky months:

Lunar March - The "sword blade" star can bring **injury or** damage to health or wealth.
Lunar June - Stars show **conflict, arguments, and money loss.**
Lunar September - Stars this month can bring **possible accidents, illness, or waste of resources.**

24

6. Snake in 2022

Born in 1929, 1941, 1953, 1965, 1985, 1977, 1989, 2001, 2013

Lucky stars for snakes in 2022 include **"Tai Yin"** (太陰) and **"Yu Tang"** (玉堂). They can bring **helpful people, happiness, and career promotion.**

The Tai Yin star is better for females. Male snakes need to pay attention to avoid relationship issues.

Negative stars include "Gou Jiao" (勾絞), "6 Harms" (六害), "Tian Guan" (天官), "Wang Shen" (亡神)... **There is an increased chance of being tricked or deceived by jealous friends this year. Watch out for** *petty people (Xiao Ren)* bringing trouble behind you.

It is a good year to **learn new skills** and maintain a good **exercise routine.**

3 lucky months:

Lunar January - 2 lucky stars (天德, 福德) bring you **helpful people, career success and fame.**
Lunar August - The "3-harmony" (三合) star brings **increased income, fame, and success.**
Lunar November - 2 lucky stars (紫微, 龍德) bring **increased income and happiness.**

3 unlucky months:

Lunar March - Watch out for **relationship trouble and illness.** Avoid argument.
Lunar April - Possible **money loss, illness, and accident.** Watch out for negative friends (Xiao Ren).
Lunar October - A star shows **wasting and decrease in money or resources** Watch for **travel safety.**

25

7. Horse in 2022

Born in 1930, 1942, (1954,) 1966, 1978, 1990, 2002, 2014

Lucky stars for horses in 2022 include "San He" (3-harmony, 三合), "Jiang Xing" (generals, 將星), "Jin Gui" (golden cabinet, 金櫃)... These stars can bring **promotion, career success, fame, power, intelligence, and increased wealth luck. It is a good year for scholars, writers, or students.**

The negative stars include "Wu Gui" (five ghosts, 五鬼), "Guan Fu" (Official Note, 官符) and so on. They are related to **legal problems, lawsuits, fighting, and accidents.**

Overall, this is a lucky year for horses. Avoid impulsive arguments or fighting to stay away from trouble.

3 lucky months:

Lunar February - Several lucky stars this month bring **happiness and money luck.**
Lunar August - *"Peach blossom star"* brings **relationship luck and festive events.**
Lunar October - Helpful people luck, business success, fame, and **increased income.**

3 unlucky months:

Lunar April - An illness star can bring **health issues.** Watch out for **legal trouble.**
Lunar July - *The "Funeral Gate" star* can bring **health issues.** Avoid attending funerals or visiting sick patients this month.
Lunar November - *The "Big Waste" star* can bring **money loss or accidents.**

8. Goat in 2022

Born in 1931, 1943, 1955, (1967, 1979,) 1991, 2003, 2015

In 2022, lucky stars for Goat include "Yue De" (月德)   and "Tian Xi" (天喜).   They ensure a year of peace, success, and wealth. You can expect festive events in the family.

Negative stars include "Si Fu" (死符)   and "Xiao Hao" (小耗).   They are related to **conflict, legal trouble, illness, or a minor decrease in wealth.**

Be careful not to listen to gossip or wrong information. For important decisions, double-check the facts carefully. Consult with experienced people.

Pay attention to your **health** and **avoid conflict or arguments.**

3 lucky months:

Lunar January - Many lucky stars bring **good fortune, and wealth luck.**
Lunar March - *"Tian De" and "Fu De"* (天德,   福德)   *stars* bring **happy events and helpful people.**
Lunar May - *"The Six-harmony star"* brings **prosperity and happiness.**

3 unlucky months:

Lunar June - *"The Sword-blade star"* can cause **accidents, illness, or money loss.**
Lunar August - Watch out for **travel safety and legal issues.** Avoid visiting **sick patients or funeral homes.**
Lunar December - The *"Big Waste"* star can cause **illness, obstacles, or money wasted.**

Paul Robertshaw-Wood
Tracey.
In Clash
Karen Jones ✓

9. Monkey in 2022

Born in 1932, 1944, 1956, 1968, 1980, 1992, 2004, 2016

Lucky stars for Monkeys in 2022 include **"Tian Jie"** (天解), **Di Jie** (地解), **Tian Ma"** (天馬), **Yi Ma"** (驛馬), and so on.

These stars bring **intelligence, promotion, fame, good health, and happy events.** Problems will be resolved or lessened this year.

"Yi Ma" (Travel Horse) is a traveling star. Monkeys have an increased chance of traveling in 2022.

One big negative star is **"Sui Po"** (歲破) because you are in the opposite direction of the Tiger, the position of **"Tai Sui"** (太歲) in 2022. This could bring **more ups and downs this year.** Stay conservative about money management and avoid risky business.

Other negative stars include **"Xue Ren"** (血刃) and **"Fu Chen"** (浮沉). Watch out for **accidents, injuries, or illnesses.** Stay flexible with your plans.

3 lucky months:

Lunar February - 2 lucky stars, **"Zi Wei", "Long De"** (紫微, 龍德), bring **increased income and happy events.**
Lunar April - The **"6-harmony"** (六合) and **"Gui Ren"** (貴人) stars bring **promotion, helpful people, and relationship luck.**
Lunar December - The **"Yue De"** (月德) and **"Tian Xi"** (天喜) stars bring **happiness and success.**

3 unlucky months:

Lunar January - The **"Da Hao"** (大耗, Big waste) star can bring **money loss and illness.**
Lunar July - Conflicting energy brings you **stress and possible illness.**
Lunar September - The **"San Men"** (Funeral gate, 喪門) star can bring **health issues, gossip, or argument.**

10. Rooster in 2022

Born in 1933, 1945, 1957, 1969, 1981, 1993, 2005, 2017

Lucky stars for Roosters in 2022 include **"Zi Wei"** (紫微), **"Long De"**(龍德), **"GuiRen"**(貴人), **"DengKe"**(登科), **"FuLu"**(福祿) and so on. They can bring **helpful people, promotion, career success, and prosperity.** You can expect increased wealth and happy events in 2022.

Negative stars include **"Bao Bai"** (暴敗), **"Tian Er"** (天噩), **"Po Sui"** (破碎)... Watch out for **safety when traveling. Avoid gossip, arguments, or fighting with others.**

Take good care of your **health.** Be patient and **avoid any risky investment.**

3 lucky months:

Lunar January - "Yue De" (月德) star brings you **increased income and business luck.**
Lunar June - **Helpful people, fame, and power** this month.
Lunar December - "San He" stars (三合, Three harmonies) bring **promotion, fame, and money luck.**

3 unlucky months:

Lunar February - The **"Da Hao"** (大耗, Big waste) star can **affect your health or finance.**
Lunar July - Watch out for **travel safety, illness,** and the tendency for **legal trouble.**
Lunar August - Increase chances of **illness or accidents.**

11. Dog in 2022

Born in 1934, 1946, 1958, 1970, 1982, 1994, 2006, 2018

Lucky stars for Dog in 2022 include **"San He" (3-harmony,** 三合**)**, **"Hua Gai"** (華蓋), **"Sui Dean"** (歲殿)**...** These stars bring artistic talent, intelligence, fame, and wealth luck. In 2022, it will be easy for dogs to **develop artistic talent and be recognized.**

One main negative star is **"Bai Hu"** (白虎, **white tiger)**. It can bring **relationship issues, gossip, or trouble from negative friends** (Xiao Ren).

Other negative stars include **"Da Sha"** (大煞, **Big Sha)** and **"Gu Xu"** (孤虛, **Alone and empty)** stars. You might feel **more lonely** this year. Be careful about **investments** with others. **Avoid gossip** and **negative friends.**

3 lucky months:

Lunar April - **"Long De"** (龍德) and **"Hong Luan"** (紅鸞, **Romance luck)** stars bring **marriage and romance luck.**
Lunar May - **"San He"** (三合) and **"Jing Gui"** (金櫃) stars bring **helpful people and increase money luck.**
Lunar October - **"Tai Yang"** (太陽), **"Gui Ren"** (貴人), and **"Tian Xi"** (天喜) stars **bring festive events and increased income.**

3 unlucky months:

Lunar March - **"Kung Po"** (空破) star can bring **obstacles or money loss.**
Lunar September - **"Jian Feng"** (Sword blade) star can increase the chance of **accident or injury.**
Lunar December - **"Gou Jiao"** (鉤絞) *star can bring increased worry and anxiety.*

狗

12. Pig in 2022

Born in 1923, 1935, 1947, 1959, 1971, 1983, 1995, 2007, 2019

In 2022, lucky stars for Pig include **"Fu De"** (福德), **"Tian De"** (天德), **"Fu Xing"** (福星), **"Sui He"** (歲合) and so on. You will have a **happy relationship** and **helpful people around you** this year. Being popular brings you **career success and increased income.**

Negative stars include **"Juan She"** (捲舌) and **"Jiao Sha"** (絞殺), **"Jie Sha"** (劫殺) and so on. The stars indicate trouble coming from gossip or words. **Avoid quarrel, fighting, and be conservative about money management.**

Pay extra attention to your **health and travel safety** in 2022.

3 lucky months:

Lunar March - **"Chang She"** (長生), **"Yue De"** (月德), and **"Hong Luan"** (紅鸞) stars bring **fame, wealth, and happy relationships**
Lunar May - **"Long De"** (龍德) *stars* bring **money luck and prosperity.**
Lunar November - **"Tai Yang"** (太陽) star brings **helpful people and career success.**

3 unlucky months:

Lunar April - **"Yue Po"** (月破) star can cause **illness or money loss.**
Lunar August - **"Tian Gou"** (天狗) star can bring **illness or legal trouble.**
Lunar October - **"Di Sha"** (地殺), **"Xue Guang"** (血光) stars can increase the chance of **accidents or money loss.**

How to use the Feng Shui calendar

The most popular information in a lunar Feng Shui calendar is **the lucky and unlucky activities of the day.** It is mainly based on the old Chinese astrology, including **the old 28 stars and 12 stars systems.**

You can also find the combinations of the 10 Heavenly stems and 12 Earthly branches timing system for each date and month. It is also called **the "Na Yin"** in Chinese. The **belonging five-element of each day** is also included. These are useful references if you practice Chinese fortune-telling or Feng Shui.

In the weekly calendar, you can find **the happiness and wealth star directions of the day.** Those are the lucky directions that could bring happiness and wealth for the day. You can use the information to plan your trip, select a seat for a meeting, or anyway you like.

There is a conflicting direction and animal sign each day. This is useful for planning major events or major construction.

Date selection basics

To select a lucky date to move, getting married, setting up a feng shui cure and so on, **first check the lucky and unlucky activities of the day.** Ideally, it should be in the list of the lucky daily activities. At least, it should not be in the unlucky activities list.

Second, check the animal signs of the major persons involved. If your animal sign is in conflict with the day, this day should be avoided.

For renovations, check the conflicting direction of the day too. Pick a starting day that is not conflicting with the direction of the construction. The first day of the construction is the most important. It is best to check the animal signs of the owner and major people involved so their signs are not conflicted.

The 24 solar terms

These 24 dates are related to farming and change of seasons. There are 2 solar terms each month. The first one indicates the beginning of the Feng Shui month. For traditional Chinese metaphysics such as Feng Shui or fortune-telling, the solar terms are used instead of just the lunar calendar. Check the next page for the list of the 24 solar terms.

The Monthly Flying Star Chart

There is a monthly Flying Star chart on each monthly pages. To learn more, Please visit **the PictureHealer YouTube channel** for the monthly Flying Star Feng Shui analysis.

The last part - Planner Pages

The last part of this book include planner pages for you to write down your monthly, yearly, and 10-year long term plans. If you put down your goals and action plans on the paper, you will have much higher chance of reaching your goals.

Activities Explained

Below are some common activities listed in this calendar. The list has been modified for modern days. Since our society is very different from the ancient times, you can be more flexible when applying these activities to the daily life.

Construction related:

- **Starting a construction** (the first day of starting a construction is important. Also check the direction of the job site and the conflicting direction of the day).
- **Setting up a door, stove, or bed** (These are for first moving to a new house, or relocating later for Feng Shui or other reasons.)
- **Moving to a new house**
- **Fixing a street, walkway, or fixing animal houses** (These are usually done on a less auspicious day.)
- **Demolition** (Some days are not lucky for almost anything, but usually good for Demolition of a building.)

Wedding related:

- **Wedding** (Ceremony or party.)
- **Dressmaking** (Making formal dress for special events.)
- **Setting up a bed** (Setting up a bed for master bedroom.)
- **Signing a contract** (This can be a lucky date for engagement.)

Religious ceremony:

- **Ceremony** (any ritual, praying, or temple visit.)
- **Activating /Removing Feng Shui cures** (a formal setting or removing of Feng Shui items requires a religious ritual.)

Funeral related:

- **Funeral** (This used to consist of many complicated steps in the old days. Now it can mean the ceremony, burial, or related activities.)
- **House cleaning** (This includes a major cleaning after a funeral.)

Business related:

- **Starting a business** (This can mean a grand opening of a store or re-opening for business after long holidays.)
- **Trading** (It can be closing of a real estate deal, stock trading, or any types of business trading.)
- **Signing a contract** (signing any legal document.)

Daily life:

- **Travel** (usually for a long distance travel)
- **Bath** (usually means purifying the body to prepare for a religious ceremony)
- **Haircut** (usually means a baby's first haircut, hair shaving for monks, or haircut for women with very long hair. You can also use the lucky haircut dates for regular haircut.)
- **Meeting friends** (meeting or family gathering for party or business purpose.)

Farming and Herding:

- **Planting** (farming)
- **Fishing**
- **Hunting**
- **Adopting animals** (Acquiring live stocks or pets)
- **Training animals** (Training farm animals to do their work.)

Activities Explained

Others:

- **Pest control**
- **Visiting a doctor**
- **Sharp knives** (Some days are marked with "sharp knives". Be careful using any tools or operating machines in those days.)
- **Avoid visiting sick patients** (In the old days, the disease could spread easily with poor hygiene. Avoid visiting sick patients on those days if your immune system is compromised. The exception is for visiting close family members. Use common sense to reduce the risk.)

Please visit **www.Picturehealer.com**

and **PictureHealer YouTube channel**

To learn more about Feng Shui and Chinese fortune telling.

2022 January

To

2023 February

Monthly and Weekly

January

Lunar December: Xin chou 辛丑 month

Monthly Flying Star chart for January 2022: January 05 to February 04

	S	
2	7	9
1	3	5
6	8	4

E (left) W (right) N (bottom)

Sunday	Monday	Tuesday	Wednesday
26 (11/23) December	27 (11/24)	28 (11/25)	29 (11/26)
2 (11/30/21)	3 (12/01/21)	4 (12/02/21)	5 (12/03/21) *Lesser Cold (Xiao Han 小寒)*
9 (12/07/21)	10 (12/08/21)	11 (12/09/21)	12 (12/10/21)
16 (12/14/21)	17 (12/15)	18 (12/16)	19 (12/17)
23 (12/21)	24 (12/22)	25 (12/23)	26 (12/24)
30 (12/28)	31 (12/29)	1 (01/01/22) Lunar New Year January	2 (01/02/22)

Monthly goals

Thursday	Friday	Saturday	Notes
30 (11/27)	31 (11/28)	1 (lunar date: 11/29/2021)	Week 1
6 (12/04/21)	7 (12/05/21)	8 (12/06/21)	Week 2
13 (12/11/21)	14 (12/12/21)	15 (12/13/21)	Week 3
20 (12/18) *Greater Cold (Da Han 大寒)*	21(12/19)	22 (12/20)	Week 4
27 (12/25)	28 (12/26)	29 (12/27)	Week 5
3 (01/03/22)	3 (01/04/22)	5 (10/22)	Week 6

February

Lunar December: Ren yin 壬寅

Monthly Flying Star chart for February 2022: February 04 to March 05

S		
1	6	8
9	2	4
5	7	3

E ... W

N

Sunday	Monday	Tuesday	Wednesday
30 (12/28) January	**31** (12/29)	**1** (lunar date: 01/01/22) Lunar New Year	**2** (01/02)
6 (01/06)	**7** (01/07)	**8** (01/08)	**9** (01/09)
13 (01/13)	**14** (01/14)	**15** (01/15)	**16** (01/16)
20 (01/20)	**21** (01/21)	**22** (01/22)	**23** (01/23)
27 (01/27)	**28** (01/28)	**1** (01/29) March	**2** (01/30)

Monthly goals

Thursday	Friday	Saturday	Notes
3 (01/03)	**4** (01/04) *_* Start of Spring (Li Chun 立春)_	**5** (01/05)	Week 1
10 (01/10)	**11** (01/11)	**12** (01/12)	Week 2
17 (01/17)	**18** (01/18)	**19** (01/19) *_* Rain Water (Yu Shui 雨水)_	Week 3
24 (01/24)	**25** (01/25)	**26** (01/26)	Week 4
3 (02/01)	4 (02/02)	5 (02/03)	Week 5

March

Lunar December: Kui mao 癸卯

Monthly Flying Star chart
for March 2022:
March 05 to
April 05

```
      S
  9  5  7
E 8  1  3 W
  4  6  2
      N
```

Monthly Flying	Monday	Tuesday	Wednesday
27 (01/27) February	27 (01/28)	1 (lunar date: 01/29)	2 (01/30)
6 (02/04)	7 (02/05)	8 (02/06)	9 (02/07)
13 (02/11)	14 (02/12)	15 (02/13)	16 (02/14)
20 (02/18) * Spring Equinox (Chun Fen 春分)	21 (02/19)	22 (02/20)	23 (02/21)
27 (02/25)	28 (02/26)	29 (02/27)	30 (02/28)

Monthly goals

Thursday	Friday	Saturday	Notes
3 (02/01)	**4** (02/02)	**5** (02/03) *Insect Awake (Jing Zhi 驚蟄)*	Week 1
10 (02/08)	**11** (02/09)	**12** (02/10)	Week 2
17 (02/15)	**18** (02/16)	**19** (02/17)	Week 3
24 (02/22)	**25** (02/23)	**26** (02/24)	Week 4
31 (02/29)	1 (03/01) April	2 (03/02)	Week 5

April

Lunar December: Jia Chen 甲辰

Monthly Flying Star chart for April 2022: April 05 to May 05

	S		
	8	4	6
E	7	9	2	W
	3	5	1
		N	

Monthly Flying	Monday	Tuesday	Wednesday
27 (02/25) March	28 (02/26)	29 (02/27)	30 (02/28)
3 (03/03)	4 (03/04)	5 (03/05) *Clear and Bright (Qing Ming 清明)	6 (03/06)
10 (03/10)	11 (03/11)	12 (03/12)	13 (03/13)
17 (03/17)	18 (03/18)	19 (03/19)	20 (03/20) *Grain Rain (Gu Yu 穀雨)
24 (03/24)	25 (03/25)	26 (03/26)	27 (03/27)

Monthly goals

Thursday	Friday	Saturday	Notes
31 (02/29)	**1** (lunar date: 03/01)	**2** (03/02)	Week 1
7 (03/07)	**8** (03/08)	**9** (03/09)	Week 2
14 (03/14)	**15** (03/15)	**16** (03/16)	Week 3
21 (03/21)	**22** (03/22)	**23** (03/23)	Week 4
28 (03/28)	**29** (03/29)	**30** (03/30)	Week 5

May

Lunar December: Yi Si 乙巳

S

7	3	5
6	8	1
2	4	9

E ... W

N

Monthly Flying	Monday	Tuesday	Wednesday
1 (lunar date: 04/01)	2 (04/02)	3 (04/03)	4 (04/04)
8 (04/08)	9 (04/09)	10 (04/10)	11 (04/11)
15 (04/15)	16 (04/16)	17 (04/17)	18 (04/18)
22 (04/22)	23 (04/23)	24 (04/24)	25 (04/25)
29 (04/29)	30 (05/01)	31 (05/02)	1 (05/03) June

Monthly goals

Thursday	Friday	Saturday	Notes
5 (04/05) ** Start of Summer (Li Xia 立夏)*	**6** (04/06)	**7** (04/07)	Week 1
12 (04/12)	**13** (04/13)	**14** (04/14)	Week 2
19 (04/19)	**20** (04/20)	**21** (04/21) ** Small (Grain) Full (Xiao Man 小滿)*	Week 3
26 (04/26)	**27** (04/27)	**28** (04/28)	Week 4
1 (05/04)	2 (05/05)	3 (05/06)	Week 5

June

Lunar December: Bing Wu 丙午

Monthly Flying Star chart
for June 2022:
June 06 to
July 07

Sunday	Monday	Tuesday	Wednesday
29 (04/29) May	30 (05/01)	31 (05/02)	1 (lunar date: 05/03)
5 (05/07)	6 (05/08) * Planting Grains (Man Zhong 芒種)	7 (05/09)	8 (05/10)
12 (05/14)	13 (05/15)	14 (05/16)	15 (05/17)
19 (05/21)	20 (05/22)	21 (05/23) * Summer Solstice (Xia Zhi 夏至)	22 (05/24)
26 (05/28)	27 (05/29)	28 (05/30)	29 (06/01)

Monthly goals

Thursday	Friday	Saturday	Notes
2 (05/04)	**3** (05/05) ** Dragon Boat Festival*	**4** (05/06)	Week 1
9 (05/11)	**10** (05/12)	**11** (05/13)	Week 2
16 (05/18)	**17** (05/19)	**18** (05/20)	Week 3
23 (05/25)	**24** (05/26)	**25** (05/27)	Week 4
30 (06/02)	1 (06/03) July	2 (06/04)	Week 5

July

Lunar December: Ding Wei 丁未

	S	
5	1	3
4	6	8
9	2	7

E (left) W (right) N (bottom)

Sunday	Monday	Tuesday	Wednesday
26 (05/28) **June**	27 (05/29)	28 (05/30)	29 (06/01)
3 (06/05)	4 (06/06)	5 (06/07)	6 (06/08)
10 (06/12)	11 (06/13)	12 (06/14)	13 (06/15)
17 (06/19)	18 (06/20)	19 (06/21)	20 (06/22)
24 (06/26)	25 (06/27)	26 (06/28)	27 (06/29)
31 (07/03)	1 (07/04) **August**	2 (07/05)	3 (07/06)

Monthly goals

Thursday	Friday	Saturday	Notes
30 (06/02)	1 (lunar date: 06/03)	2 (06/04)	Week 1
7 (06/09) * *Lesser Heat (Xiao Shu 小暑)*	8 (06/10)	9 (06/11)	Week 2
14 (06/16)	15 (06/17)	16 (06/18)	Week 3
21 (06/23)	22 (06/24)	23 (06/25) * *Greater Heat (Da Shu 大暑)*	Week 4
28 (06/30)	29 (07/01)	30 (07/02)	Week 5
4 (07/07)	5 (07/08)	6 (07/09)	Week 6

August

Lunar December: Wu Shen 戊申

Monthly Flying Star chart for August 2022: August 07 to September 07

S

4	9	2
3	5	7
8	1	6

E — W

N

Sunday	Monday	Tuesday	Wednesday
31 (07/03) July	**1** (lunar date: 07/04)	**2** (07/05)	**3** (07/06)
7 (07/10) ** Start of Autumn (Li Qiu 立秋)*	**8** (07/11)	**9** (07/12)	**10** (07/13)
14 (07/17)	**15** (07/18)	**16** (07/19)	**17** (07/20)
21 (07/24)	**22** (07/25)	**23** (07/26) ** Hidden Summer (Chu Shu 處暑)*	**24** (07/27)
28 (08/02)	**29** (08/03)	**30** (08/04)	**31** (08/05)

Monthly goals

Thursday	Friday	Saturday	Notes
4 (07/07)	**5** (07/08)	**6** (07/09)	Week 1
11 (07/14)	**12** (07/15)	**13** (07/16)	Week 2
18 (07/21)	**19** (07/22)	**20** (07/23)	Week 3
25 (07/28)	**26** (07/29)	**27** (08/01)	Week 4
1 (08/06) September	2 (08/07)	3 (08/08)	Week 5

September

Lunar December: Ji You 己酉

	S	
3	8	1
2	4	6
7	9	5

E (left) · W (right) · N (bottom)

Sunday	Monday	Tuesday	Wednesday
28 (08/02) August	**29** (08/03)	**30** (08/04)	**31** (08/05)
4 (08/09)	**5** (08/10)	**6** (08/11)	**7** (08/12) * *White Dew* *(Bai Lu 白露)*
11 (08/16)	**12** (08/17)	**13** (08/18)	**14** (08/19)
18 (08/23)	**19** (08/24)	**20** (08/25)	**21** (08/26)
25 (08/30)	**26** (09/01)	**27** (09/02)	**28** (09/03)

Monthly goals

Thursday	Friday	Saturday	Notes
1 (lunar date: 08/06)	**2** (08/07)	**3** (08/08)	Week 1
8 (08/13)	**9** (08/14)	**10** (08/15) ** Moon Festival*	Week 2
15 (08/20)	**16** (08/21)	**17** (08/22)	Week 3
22 (08/27)	**23** (08/28) ** Autumn Equinox (Qiu Fen 秋分)*	**24** (08/29)	Week 4
29 (09/04)	**30** (09/05)	1 (09/06) October	Week 5

October

Lunar December: Geng Xu 庚戌

Monthly Flying Star chart for October 2022: October 08 to November 07

	S	
2	7	9
E 1	3	5 W
6	8	4
	N	

Sunday	Monday	Tuesday	Wednesday
25 (08/30) September	26 (09/01)	27 (09/02)	28 (09/03)
2 (09/07)	3 (09/08)	4 (09/09)	5 (09/10)
9 (09/14)	10 (09/15)	11 (09/16)	12 (09/17)
16 (09/21)	17 (09/22)	18 (09/23)	19 (09/24)
23 (09/28) *Frost Descent (Shung Jiang 霜降)*	24 (09/29)	25 (10/01)	26 (10/02)
30 (10/06)	31 (10/07)	1 (10/08) November	2 (10/09)

Monthly goals

Thursday	Friday	Saturday	Notes
29 (09/04)	**30** (09/05)	**1** (lunar date: 09/06)	Week 1
6 (09/11)	**7** (09/12)	**8** (09/13) ** Cold Dew (Han Lu 寒露)*	Week 2
13 (09/18)	**14** (09/19)	**15** (09/20)	Week 3
20 (09/25)	**21**(09/26)	**22** (09/27)	Week 4
27 (10/03)	**28** (10/04)	**29** (10/05)	Week 5
3 (10/10)	**4** (10/11)	**5** (10/12)	Week 6

November

Lunar December: Xin Hai 辛亥

```
          S
      1   6   8
  E   9   2   4   W
      5   7   3
          N
```

Sunday	Monday	Tuesday	Wednesday
30 (10/06) October	31 (10/07)	1 (lunar date: 10/08)	2 (10/09)
6 (10/13)	7 (10/14) *Start of Winter (Li Dong 立冬)*	8 (10/15)	9 (10/16)
13 (10/20)	14 (10/21)	15 (10/22)	16 (10/23)
20 (10/27)	21 (10/28)	22 (10/29) *Lesser Snow (Xiao Xue 小雪)*	23 (10/30)
27 (11/04)	28 (11/05)	29 (11/06)	30 (11/07)

Monthly goals

Thursday	Friday	Saturday	Notes
3 (10/10)	**4** (10/11)	**5** (10/12)	Week 1
10 (10/17)	**11** (10/18)	**12** (10/19)	Week 2
17 (10/24)	**18** (10/25)	**19** (10/26)	Week 3
24 (11/01)	**25** (11/02)	**26** (11/03)	Week 4
1 (11/08) December	2 (11/09)	3 (11/10)	Week 5

December

Lunar December: Ren Zi 壬子

	S	
9	5	7
8	1	3
4	6	2
	N	

E (left) W (right)

Sunday	Monday	Tuesday	Wednesday
27 (11/04) November	28 (11/05)	29 (11/06)	30 (11/07)
4 (11/11)	5 (11/12)	6 (11/13)	7 (11/14) *Greater Snow (Da Xue 大雪)*
11 (11/18)	12 (11/19)	13 (11/20)	14 (11/21)
18 (11/25)	19 (11/26)	20 (11/27)	21 (11/28)
25 (12/03)	26 (12/04)	27 (12/05)	28 (12/06)

Monthly goals

Thursday	Friday	Saturday	Notes
1 (lunar date: 11/08)	**2** (11/09)	**3** (11/10)	Week 1
8 (11/15)	**9** (11/16)	**10** (11/17)	Week 2
15 (11/22)	**16** (11/23)	**17** (11/24)	Week 3
22 (11/29) *Winter Solstice (Dong Zhi 冬至)*	**23** (12/01)	**24** (12/02)	Week 4
29 (12/07)	**30** (12/08)	**31** (12/09)	Week 5

January 2023

Lunar December: Kui Chou 癸丑

Monthly Flying Star chart for January 2023: January 05 to February 04, 2023

	S	
8	4	6
7	9	2
3	5	1

E (left) W (right) N (bottom)

Sunday	Monday	Tuesday	Wednesday
1 (lunar date: 12/10)	**2** (12/11)	**3** (12/12)	**4** (12/13)
8 (12/17)	**9** (12/18)	**10** (12/19)	**11** (12/20)
15 (12/24)	**16** (12/25)	**17** (12/26)	**18** (12/27)
22 (01/01/23) Lunar New Year	**23** (01/02)	**24** (01/03)	**25** (01/04)
29 (01/08)	**30** (01/09)	**31** (01/10)	1 (01/11) February

Monthly goals

Thursday	Friday	Saturday	Notes
5 (12/14) ** Lesser Cold (Xiao Han 小寒)*	**6** (12/15)	**7** (12/16)	Week 1
12 (12/21)	**13** (12/22)	**14** (12/23)	Week 2
19 (12/28)	**20** (12/29) ** Greater Cold (Da Han 大寒)*	**21** (12/30)	Week 3
26 (01/05)	**27** (01/06)	**28** (01/07)	Week 4
2 (01/12)	3 (01/13)	4 (01/14)	Week 5

February 2023

Lunar December: Jia Yin 甲寅

Monthly Flying Star chart for February 2023: February 04 to March 06, 2023

	S	
7	3	5
6	8	1
2	4	9
	N	

E (left) — W (right)

Sunday	Monday	Tuesday	Wednesday
29 (01/08/23) January	**30** (01/09)	**31** (01/10)	**1** (lunar date: 01/11)
5 (01/15)	**6** (01/16)	**7** (01/17)	**8** (01/18)
12 (01/22)	**13** (01/23)	**14** (01/24)	**15** (01/25)
19 (01/29) *Rain Water (Yu Shui 雨水)*	**20** (02/01)	**21** (02/02)	**22** (02/03)
26 (02/07)	**27** (02/08)	**28** (02/09)	**1** (02/10) March

Monthly goals

Thursday	Friday	Saturday	Notes
2 (01/12)	**3** (01/13)	**4** (01/14) ** Start of Spring (Li Chun 立春)*	Week 1
9 (01/19)	**10** (01/20)	**11** (01/21)	Week 2
16 (01/26)	**17** (01/27)	**18** (01/28)	Week 3
23 (02/04)	**24** (02/05)	**25** (02/06)	Week 4
3 (02/11)	**4** (02/12)	**5** (02/13)	Week 5

December 2021 - January 2022

Week 1

January

S	M	T	W	T	F	S
26	27	28	29	30	31	1
2	3	4	5	6	7	8
9	10	11	12	13	14	15
16	17	18	19	20	21	22
23	24	25	26	27	28	29
30	31	1	2	3	4	5

---

27 (lunar date: 11/24/2021)   **Monday**
                                                Ji You (己酉) - Earth

Happiness star: **Northeast**, Wealth star: **North**

Conflicting sign: **Rabbit** Conflicting direction: **East**

Lucky: Bath, Haircut, House cleaning, Pest control, Hunting, Planting.

Avoid: Wedding, Moving to a new house, Sharp knives.

---

28 (11/25)   **Tuesday**
                                                Geng Xu (庚戌) - Metal

Happiness star: **Northeast**, Wealth star: **East**

Conflicting sign: **Dragon,** Conflicting direction: **North**

Lucky: Ceremony, Activating Feng Shui cures, Dressmaking, Starting a construction, Setting up a door/bed, Planting, Adopting animals.

Avoid: None.

---

29 (11/26)   **Wednesday**
                                                Xin Hai (辛亥) - Metal

Happiness star: **Southwest**, Wealth star: **East**

Conflicting sign: **Snake,** Conflicting direction: **West**

Lucky: Bath, Dressmaking, Starting a construction, Setting up a door/stove, Pest control, Planting.

Avoid: Activating Feng Shui cures.

---

30 (11/27)   **Thursday**
                                                Ren Zi (壬子) - Water

Happiness star: **South**, Wealth star: **South**

Conflicting sign: **Horse** Conflicting direction: **South**

Lucky: Starting a business, Funeral.

Avoid: Wedding, Starting a construction.

Weekly goals/ to do:

_____
_____
_____
_____

---

31 (11/28)   **Friday**
                                               Kui Chou (癸丑) - Wood

Happiness star: **Northeast**, Wealth star: **Southeast**
Conflicting sign: **Goat,** Conflicting direction: **East**

Lucky: Ceremony, Travel, Wedding, Bath, Dressmaking, Starting a construction, Moving to a
new house, Starting a business, Adopting animals.
Avoid: Activating Feng Shui cures.

Jan 1, 2022 (11/29/2021) ** New Year's Day*   Saturday
                                               Jia Yin (甲寅) - Water

Happiness star: **Northeast**, Wealth star: **Southeast**
Conflicting sign: **Monkey,** Conflicting direction: **North**

Lucky: Activating Feng Shui cures, Travel, Renovation, Setting up a door/bed, Starting a
business, Trading, Planting, Funeral.
Avoid: Visiting sick patients.

---

2 (11/30)   Sunday
                                               Yi Mao (乙卯) - Water

Happiness star: **Northwest**, Wealth star: **Southeast**
Conflicting sign: **Rooster,** Conflicting direction: **West**

Lucky: Ceremony, Bath, Haircut, House cleaning, Removing Feng Shui cures.
Avoid: Any major festive event, Visiting sick patients.

Weekly review/ gratitude:

_____
_____
_____
_____
_____

January 2022

Week 2

January

S	M	T	W	T	F	S
26	27	28	29	30	31	1
2	3	4	5	6	7	8
9	10	11	12	13	14	15
16	17	18	19	20	21	22
23	24	25	26	27	28	29
30	31	1	2	3	4	5

---

3 (lunar date: 12/01/2021)   **Monday**
Bing Chen (丙辰) - Earth

Happiness star: **Southwest**, Wealth star: **West**
Conflicting sign: **Dog,** Conflicting direction: **South**

Lucky: Ceremony, Starting a construction, Setting up a bed/door, Moving to a new house, Adopting animals, Funeral.
Avoid: Setting up a stove.

---

4 (12/02)   **Tuesday**
Ding Si (丁巳) - Earth

Happiness star: **South**, Wealth star: **West**
Conflicting sign: **Pig,** Conflicting direction: **East**

Lucky: Ceremony, Hunting, Pest control.
Avoid: Wedding, Travel.

---

5 (12/03) * *Lesser Cold (Xiao Han 小寒)*   **Wednesday**
Wu Wu (戊午) - Fire

Happiness star: **Southeast**, Wealth star: **North**
Conflicting sign: **Rat,** Conflicting direction: **North**

Lucky: Ceremony, Bath, Demolition.
Avoid: Any major festive event.

---

6 (12/04)   **Thursday**
Ji Wei (己未) - Fire

Happiness star: **Northeast**, Wealth star: **North**
Conflicting sign: **Ox,** Conflicting direction: **West**

Lucky: Ceremony, Demolition.
Avoid: Any major festive event.

7 (12/05)

Friday
Geng Shen (庚申) - Wood

Happiness star: **Northwest**, Wealth star: **East**
Conflicting sign: **Tiger,** Conflicting direction: **South**

Lucky: Ceremony, Activating Feng Shui cures, Wedding, Starting a construction, Moving to a new house, Adopting animals, Funeral.
Avoid: Sharp knives.

8 (12/06)

Saturday
Xin You (辛酉) - Wood

Happiness star: **Southwest**, Wealth star: **East**
Conflicting sign: **Rabbit,** Conflicting direction: **East**

Lucky: Removing Feng Shui cures, Visiting a doctor, Funeral.
Avoid: Any major festive event. Sharp knives.

9 (12/07)

Sunday
Ren Xu (壬戌) - Water

Happiness star: **South**, Wealth star: **South**
Conflicting sign: **Dragon,** Conflicting direction: **North**

Lucky: Ceremony, Removing Feng Shui cures, Setting up a stove, Renovation, Pest control, House cleaning, Hunting, Fishing.
Avoid: Wedding, Starting a business.

Weekly review/ gratitude:

January 2022

Week 3

January

S	M	T	W	T	F	S
26	27	28	29	30	31	1
2	3	4	5	6	7	8
9	10	11	12	13	14	15
16	17	18	19	20	21	22
23	24	25	26	27	28	29
30	31	1	2	3	4	5

---

10 (lunar date: 12/08)   **Monday**
Kui Hai (癸亥) - Water

Happiness star: **Southeast**, Wealth star: **South**
Conflicting sign: **Snake**, Conflicting direction: **West**

Lucky: Activating Feng Shui cures, Bath, Haircut, Visiting a doctor, Metting friends, Setting up a stove, Fixitng animal houses.
Avoid: Moving to a new house.

---

11 (12/09)   **Tuesday**
Jia Zi (甲子) - Metal

Happiness star: **Northeast**, Wealth star: **Southeast**
Conflicting sign: **Horse**, Conflicting direction: **South**

Lucky: Ceremony, Renovation, Setting up a bed/stove.
Avoid: Wedding, Moving to a new house.

---

12 (12/10)   **Wednesday**
Yi Chou (乙丑) - Metal

Happiness star: **Northwest**, Wealth star: **Southeast**
Conflicting sign: **Goat**, Conflicting direction: **East**

Lucky: Ceremony, Removing Feng Shui cures, Meeting friends.
Avoid: Any major festive event.

---

13 (12/11)   **Thursday**
Bing Yin (丙寅) - Fire

Happiness star: **Southwest**, Wealth star: **West**
Conflicting sign: **Monkey**, Conflicting direction: **North**

Lucky: Dressmaking, Wedding, Starting a construction, Setting up a bed, Moving to a new house, Trading, Funeral.
Avoid: Ceremony.

---

14 (12/12)

Friday
Ding Mao (丁卯) - Fire

Happiness star: **South**, Wealth star: **West**
Conflicting sign: **Rooster,** Conflicting direction: **West**

Lucky: Ceremony, Travel, Signing a contract, Dressmaking, Wedding, Meeting friends, Setting up a bed, Starting a business, Trading, Planting, Funeral.
Avoid: None.

---

15 (12/13)

Saturday
Wu Chen (戊辰) - Wood

Happiness star: **Southeast**, Wealth star: **North**
Conflicting sign: **Dog,** Conflicting direction: **South**

Lucky: Ceremony, Renovation, Fixing a street/walkway.
Avoid: Setting up a stove.

---

16 (12/14)

Sunday
Ji Si (己巳) - Wood

Happiness star: **Northeast**, Wealth star: **North**
Conflicting sign: **Pig,** Conflicting direction: **East**

Lucky: Ceremony, Activating Feng Shui cures, Wedding, Meeting friends, Starting a construction, Setting up a bed/stove, Moving to a new house, Adopting animals.
Avoid: Travel.

Weekly review/ gratitude:

January 2022

Week 4

January

S	M	T	W	T	F	S
26	27	28	29	30	31	1
2	3	4	5	6	7	8
9	10	11	12	13	14	15
16	17	18	19	20	21	22
23	24	25	26	27	28	29
30	31	1	2	3	4	5

---

17 (lunar date: 12/15)

Monday
Geng Wu (庚午) - Earth

Happiness star: **Northwest**, Wealth star: **East**

Conflicting sign: **Rat**, Conflicting direction: **North**

Lucky: Ceremony, Travel, Setting up a bed, Adopting animals, Funeral.

Avoid: Moving to a new house, Visiting sick patients.

---

18 (12/16)

Tuesday
Xin Wei (辛未) - Earth

Happiness star: **Southwest**, Wealth star: **East**

Conflicting sign: **Ox**, Conflicting direction: **West**

Lucky: Ceremony, Demolition, Removing Feng Shui cures.

Avoid: Any major festive event.

---

19 (12/17)

Wednesday
Ren Shen (壬申) - Metal

Happiness star: **South**, Wealth star: **South**

Conflicting sign: **Tiger**, Conflicting direction: **South**

Lucky: Ceremony, Travel, Starting a business, Trading, Hunting, Adopting animals.

Avoid: Sharp knives.

---

20 (12/18) ** Greater Cold (Da Han 大寒)*

Thursday
Kui You (癸酉) - Metal

Happiness star: **Southeast**, Wealth star: **South**

Conflicting sign: **Rabbit**, Conflicting direction: **East**

Lucky: Ceremony, Removing Feng Shui cures.

Avoid: Any major festive event, sharp knives.

---

21 (12/19)

Friday
Jia Wu (甲戌) - Fire

Happiness star: **Northeast**, Wealth star: **Southeast**
Conflicting sign: **Dragon**, Conflicting direction: **North**

Lucky: Ceremony, Dressmaking, Wedding, Setting up a stove, Hunting, Planting.
Avoid: Starting a business.

---

22 (12/20)

Saturday
Yi Hai (乙亥) - Fire

Happiness star: **Northwest**, Wealth star: **Southeast**
Conflicting sign: **Snake,** Conflicting direction: **West**

Lucky: Ceremony, Activating Feng Shui cures, Dressmaking, Renovation, Setting up a bed/stove, Moving to a new house, Trading.
Avoid: Wedding.

---

23 (12/21)

Sunday
Bing Zi (丙子) - Water

Happiness star: **Southwest**, Wealth star: **West**
Conflicting sign: **Horse,** Conflicting direction: **South**

Lucky: Ceremony, Bath, Dressmaking, Setting up a bed, Trading, Funeral.
Avoid: Wedding, Setting up a stove.

Weekly review/ gratitude:

January 2022

Week 5

January

S	M	T	W	T	F	S
26	27	28	29	30	31	1
2	3	4	5	6	7	8
9	10	11	12	13	14	15
16	17	18	19	20	21	22
23	24	25	26	27	28	29
30	31	1	2	3	4	5

---

24 (lunar date: 12/22)   **Monday**
                                                       Ding Chou (丁丑) - Water

Happiness star: **South**, Wealth star: **West**

Conflicting sign: **Goat**, Conflicting direction: **East**

Lucky: Ceremony, Removing Feng Shui cures, Visiting a doctor, Training animals.
Avoid: Any major festive event.

---

25 (12/23)   **Tuesday**
                                                       Wu Yin (戊寅) - Earth

Happiness star: **Southeast**, Wealth star: **North**

Conflicting sign: **Monkey**, Conflicting direction: **North**

Lucky: Dressmaking, Renovation, Setting up a bed, Moving to a new house, Starting a business, Trading, Adopting animals, Funeral.
Avoid: Ceremony.

---

26 (12/24)   **Wednesday**
                                                       Ji Mao (己卯) - Earth

Happiness star: **Northeast**, Wealth star: **North**

Conflicting sign: **Rooster**, Conflicting direction: **West**

Lucky: Ceremony, Dressmaking, Wedding, Meeting friends, Setting up a bed, Starting a business, Trading, Pest control, Adopting animals.
Avoid: Setting up a stove.

---

27 (12/25)   **Thursday**
                                                       Geng Chen (庚辰) - Metal

Happiness star: **Northwest**, Wealth star: **East**

Conflicting sign: **Dog**, Conflicting direction: **South**

Lucky: Ceremony, Setting up a bed, Renovation, Fixing a street/walkway, Funeral.
Avoid: Setting up a stove.

Weekly goals/ to do:

---

28 (12/26)   **Friday**
                                                          Xin Si (辛巳) - Metal
Happiness star: **Southwest**, Wealth star: **East**
Conflicting sign: **Pig** Conflicting direction: **East**

Lucky: Ceremony, Starting a class, Signing a contract, Wedding, Meeting friends, Adopting animals.
Avoid: Travel, Moving to a new house.

---

29 (12/27)   Saturday
                                                          Ren Wu (壬午) - Wood
Happiness star: **South**, Wealth star: **South**
Conflicting sign: **Rat,** Conflicting direction: **North**

Lucky: Ceremony, Travel, Bath, Dressmaking, Wedding, Renovation, Setting up a bed, Moving to a new house, Hunting, Funeral.
Avoid: Visiting sick patients.

---

30 (12/28)   Sunday
                                                          Kui Wei (癸未) - Wood
Happiness star: **Southeast**, Wealth star: **South**
Conflicting sign: **Ox,** Conflicting direction: **West**

Lucky: Ceremony, Demolition.
Avoid: Any major festive event.

Weekly review/ gratitude:

January - February 2022

Week 6

February

S	M	T	W	T	F	S
30	31	1	2	3	4	5
6	7	8	9	10	11	12
13	14	15	16	17	18	19
20	21	22	23	24	25	26
27	28	1	2	3	4	5

---

31 (lunar date: 12/29)

Monday
Jia Shen (甲申) - Water

Happiness star: **Northeast,** Wealth star: **Southeast**

Conflicting sign: **Tiger** Conflicting direction: **South**

Lucky: Ceremony, Activating Feng Shui cures, Travel, Wedding, Renovation, Moving to a new house, Starting a business, Adopting animals, Funeral.

Avoid: Sharp knives.

Feb 1 (01/01/2022) * *Lunar New Year*

Tuesday
Yi You (乙酉) - Water

Happiness star: **Northwest,** Wealth star: **Southeast**

Conflicting sign: **Rabbit,** Conflicting direction: **East**

Lucky: Ceremony, Bath, House cleaning, Funeral.

Avoid: Any major festive event, sharp knives.

---

2 (01/02)

Wednesday
Bing Wu (丙戌) - Earth

Happiness star: **Southwest,** Wealth star: **West**

Conflicting sign: **Dragon,** Conflicting direction: **North**

Lucky: Ceremony, Wedding, Hunting.

Avoid: Starting a business.

---

3 (01/03)

Thursday
Ding Hai (丁亥) - Earth

Happiness star: **South,** Wealth star: **West**

Conflicting sign: **Snake,** Conflicting direction: **West**

Lucky: Ceremony, Activating Feng Shui cures, Dressmaking, Starting a business, Trading, Adopting animals.

Avoid: Wedding, Setting up a stove.

Weekly goals/ to do:

_____

_____

_____

_____

_____

---

4 (01/04) * *Start of Spring (Li Chun 立春)*   **Friday**
Happiness star: **Southeast**, Wealth star: **North**   Wu Zi (戊子) - Fire
Conflicting sign: **Horse** Conflicting direction: **South**

Lucky: Ceremony, Activating Feng Shui cures, Dressmaking, Meeting friends, Renovation, Starting a business, Trading, Planting.
Avoid: Sharp knives.

---

5 (01/05)   Saturday
Happiness star: **Northeast**, Wealth star: **North**   Ji Chou (己丑) - Fire
Conflicting sign: **Goat,** Conflicting direction: **East**

Lucky: Ceremony, Dressmaking, Setting up a bed/stove, Pest control.
Avoid: Wedding.

---

6 (01/06)   Sunday
Happiness star: **Northwest**, Wealth star: **East**   Geng Ying (庚寅) - Wood
Conflicting sign: **Monkey,** Conflicting direction: **North**

Lucky: Wedding, Dressmaking, Meeting friends, Starting a business, Trading, Funeral.
Avoid: Travel.

Weekly review/ gratitude:

_____

_____

_____

_____

February 2022

Week 7

February

S	M	T	W	T	F	S
30	31	1	2	3	4	5
6	7	8	9	10	11	12
13	14	15	16	17	18	19
20	21	22	23	24	25	26
27	28	1	2	3	4	5

---

7 (lunar date: 01/07)   **Monday**
Xin Mao (辛卯) - Wood

Happiness star: **Southwest**, Wealth star: **East**
Conflicting sign: **Rooster**, Conflicting direction: **West**

Lucky: Ceremony, Travel, Setting up a bed, Moving to a new house, Funeral.
Avoid: Setting up a stove.

---

8 (01/08)   **Tuesday**
Ren Chen (壬辰) - Water

Happiness star: **South**, Wealth star: **South**
Conflicting sign: **Dog**, Conflicting direction: **South**

Lucky: Travel, Wedding, Meeting friends, Moving, Trading, Adopting animals.
Avoid: None.

---

9 (01/09)   **Wednesday**
Kui Si (癸巳) - Water

Happiness star: **Southeast**, Wealth star: **South**
Conflicting sign: **Pig,** Conflicting direction: **East**

Lucky: Setting up a stove, Fixing a street/walkway.
Avoid: Travel.

---

10 (01/10)   **Thursday**
Jia Wu (甲午) - Metal

Happiness star: **Northeast,** Wealth star: **Southeast**
Conflicting sign: **Rat,** Conflicting direction: **North**

Lucky: Ceremony, Dressmaking, Starting a construction, Setting up a bed, Starting a business, Adopting animals, Fixing animal houses.
Avoid: Funeral, Setting up a stove.

---

11 (01/11)

Happiness star: **Northwest**, Wealth star: **Southeast**

Conflicting sign: **Ox,** Conflicting direction: **West**

Friday

Yi Wei (乙未) - Metal

Lucky: Ceremony, Dressmaking, Wedding, Setting up a bed, Hunting, Fishing, Funeral.

Avoid: None.

---

12 (01/12)

Happiness star: **Southwest**, Wealth star: **West**

Conflicting sign: **Tiger,** Conflicting direction: **South**

Saturday

Bing Shen (丙申) - Fire

Lucky: Ceremony, Removing Feng Shui cures, Bath, Visiting a doctor, Demolition, House cleaning.

Avoid: Setting up a bed/stove.

---

13 (01/13)

Happiness star: **South**, Wealth star: **West**

Conflicting sign: **Rabbit,** Conflicting direction: **East**

Sunday

Ding You (丁酉) - Fire

Lucky: Ceremony, Travel, Starting a construction, Starting a business, Planting, Adopting animals, Funeral.

Avoid: None.

Weekly review/ gratitude:

February 2022

Week 8

February

S	M	T	W	T	F	S
30	31	1	2	3	4	5
6	7	8	9	10	11	12
13	14	15	16	17	18	19
20	21	22	23	24	25	26
27	28	1	2	3	4	5

---

14 (lunar date: 01/14)   **Monday**
                                                        Wu Xu (戊戌) - Wood

Happiness star: **Southeast**, Wealth star: **North**

Conflicting sign: **Dragon**, Conflicting direction: **North**

Lucky: Pest control, Fishing, Funeral.

Avoid: Any major festive event.

---

15 (01/15)   **Tuesday**
                                                        Ji Hai (己亥) - Wood

Happiness star: **Northeast**, Wealth star: **North**

Conflicting sign: **Snake**, Conflicting direction: **West**

Lucky: Ceremony, Bath, Haircut, Signing a contract, Dressmaking, Setting up a bed, Planting, Adopting animals.

Avoid: None.

---

16 (01/16)   **Wednesday**
                                                        Geng Zi (庚子) - Earth

Happiness star: **Northwest**, Wealth star: **East**

Conflicting sign: **Horse**, Conflicting direction: **South**

Lucky: Ceremony, Activating Feng Shui cures, Starting a class, Travel, Bath, Haircut, Dressmaking, Wedding, Starting a business, Trading.

Avoid: None.

---

17 (01/17)   **Thursday**
                                                        Xin Chou (辛丑) - Earth

Happiness star: **Southwest**, Wealth star: **East**

Conflicting sign: **Goat**, Conflicting direction: **East**

Lucky: Ceremony.

Avoid: Wedding, Moving to a new house.

18 (01/18)   **Friday**
                                                              Ren Ying (壬寅) - Metal

Happiness star: **South**, Wealth star: **South**
Conflicting sign: **Monkey,** Conflicting direction: **North**

Lucky: Dressmaking, Meeting friends, Setting up a bed, Starting a business, Trading, Adopting animals, Funeral.
Avoid: None.

19 (01/19) ** Rain Water (Yu Shui 雨水)*   Saturday
                                                              Kui Mao (癸卯) - Metal

Happiness star: **Southeast**, Wealth star: **South**
Conflicting sign: **Rooster,** Conflicting direction: **West**

Lucky: Ceremony, Activating Feng Shui cures, Travel, Wedding, Starting a construction, Setting up a bed, Moving to a new house, Starting a business, Adopting animals, Funeral.
Avoid: None.

20 (01/20)   Sunday
                                                              Jia Chen (甲辰) - Fire

Happiness star: **Northeast**, Wealth star: **Southeast**
Conflicting sign: **Dog,** Conflicting direction: **South**

Lucky: Ceremony, Activating Feng Shui cures, Visiting a doctor, Wedding, Meeting friends, Setting up a bed.
Avoid: Building a temple.

Weekly review/ gratitude:

February 2022

Week 9

February

S	M	T	W	T	F	S
30	31	1	2	3	4	5
6	7	8	9	10	11	12
13	14	15	16	17	18	19
20	21	22	23	24	25	26
27	28	1	2	3	4	5

---

21 (lunar date: 01/21)

Monday
Yi Si (乙巳) - Fire

Happiness star: **Northwest**, Wealth star: **Southeast**
Conflicting sign: **Pig**, Conflicting direction: **East**

Lucky: Setting up a stove, Fixing a street/walkway.
Avoid: Funeral.

---

22 (01/22)

Tuesday
Bing Wu (丙午) - Water

Happiness star: **Southwest**, Wealth star: **West**
Conflicting sign: **Rat**, Conflicting direction: **North**

Lucky: Ceremony, Travel, Wedding, Starting a construction, Setting up a bed, Moving to a new house, Starting a business, Planting, Adopting animals, Funeral.
Avoid: None.

---

23 (01/23)

Wednesday
Ding Wei (丁未) - Water

Happiness star: **South**, Wealth star: **West**
Conflicting sign: **Ox**, Conflicting direction: **West**

Lucky: Ceremony, Travel, Dressmaking, Starting a construction, Setting up a bed, Moving to a new house, Planting, Adopting animals, Funeral.
Avoid: None.

---

24 (01/24)

Thursday
Wu Shen (戊申) - Earth

Happiness star: **Southeast**, Wealth star: **North**
Conflicting sign: **Tiger**, Conflicting direction: **South**

Lucky: Ceremony, Removing Feng Shui cures, Bath, Visiting a doctor, Demolition, House cleaning.
Avoid: Any major festive event.

25 (01/25)

Friday
Ji You (己酉) - Earth

Happiness star: **Northeast**, Wealth star: **North**
Conflicting sign: **Rabbit,** Conflicting direction: **East**

Lucky: Ceremony, Activating Feng Shui cures, Travel, Dressmaking, Starting a construction, Starting a business, Funeral.
Avoid: None.

26 (01/26)

Saturday
Geng Xu (庚戌) - Metal

Happiness star: **Northwest**, Wealth star: **East**
Conflicting sign: **Dragon** Conflicting direction: **North**

Lucky: Starting a class, Pest control, Funeral.
Avoid: Any major festive event, Wedding.

27 (01/27)

Sunday
Xin Hai (辛亥) - Metal

Happiness star: **Southwest**, Wealth star: **East**
Conflicting sign: **Snake,** Conflicting direction: **West**

Lucky: Ceremony, Activating Feng Shui cures, Travel, Starting a construction, Setting up a bed/ stove, Moving to a new house, Starting a business, Training animals, Adopting animals, Planting.
Avoid: None.

Weekly review/ gratitude:

February - March 2022

Week 10

March

S	M	T	W	T	F	S
27	28	1	2	3	4	5
6	7	8	9	10	11	12
13	14	15	16	17	18	19
20	21	22	23	24	25	26
27	28	29	30	31	1	2

---

28 (lunar date: 01/28)　　　　　　　　　**Monday**
Ren Zi (壬子) - Wood

Happiness star: **South**,　Wealth star: **South**
Conflicting sign: **Horse,**　Conflicting direction: **South**

Lucky: Ceremony, Activating Feng Shui cures, Haircut, Dressmaking, Wedding, Starting a construction, Setting up a bed, Planting, Adopting animals.
Avoid: None.

Mar 1 (01/29)　　　　　　　　　　　**Tuesday**
Kui Chou (癸丑) - Wood

Happiness star: **Southeast**,　Wealth star: **South**
Conflicting sign: **Goat,**　Conflicting direction: **East**

Lucky: Ceremony, Dressmaking, Visiting a doctor, Setting up a bed/stove, Funeral.
Avoid: Moving to a new house.

---

2 (01/30)　　　　　　　　　　　**Wednesday**
Jia Yin (甲寅) - Water

Happiness star: **Northeast**　Wealth star: **Northeast**
Conflicting sign: **Monkey,**　Conflicting direction: **North**

Lucky: Dressmaking, Trading.
Avoid: Any major festive event.

---

3 (02/01)　　　　　　　　　　　**Thursday**
Yi Mao (乙卯) - Water

Happiness star: **Northwest**,　Wealth star: **Northeast**
Conflicting sign: **Rooster,**　Conflicting direction: **West**

Lucky: Starting a construction, Moving to a new house, Setting up a bed, Starting a business, Trading, Funeral.
Avoid: None.

Weekly goals/ to do:

---

4 (02/02)

Happiness star: **Southwest**, Wealth star: **West**

Conflicting sign: **Dog,,** Conflicting direction: **South**

Friday
Bing Chen (丙辰) - Earth

Lucky: Ceremony, Wedding, Travel, Meeting friends, Setting up a bed/door, Hunting, Activating Feng Shui cures, Renovation.

Avoid: Moving to a new house, Setting up a bed, Funeral.

---

5 (02/03) * *Insect Awake (Jing Zhi 驚蟄)*

Happiness star: **South**, Wealth star: **West**

Conflicting sign: **Pig,** Conflicting direction: **East**

Saturday
Ding Si (丁巳) - Earth

Lucky: Activating Feng Shui cures, Signing a contract, Dressmaking, Meeting friends, Starting a business, Trading, Setting up a bed, Planting.

Avoid: Travel, Moving to a new house, Funeral, Setting up a stove.

---

6 (02/04)

Happiness star: **Southeast**, Wealth star: **North**

Conflicting sign: **Rat,** Conflicting direction: **North**

Sunday
Wu Wu (戊午) - Fire

Lucky: Ceremony, Wedding.

Avoid: Starting a construction, Setting up a stove/bed, Moving to a new house, Activating Feng Shui cures.

Weekly review/ gratitude:

March 2022

Week 11

March

S	M	T	W	T	F	S
27	28	1	2	3	4	5
6	7	8	9	10	11	12
13	14	15	16	17	18	19
20	21	22	23	24	25	26
27	28	29	30	31	1	2

---

7 (lunar date: 02/05)

Monday
Ji Wei (己未) - Fire

Happiness star: **Northeast**, Wealth star: **North**
Conflicting sign: **Ox**, Conflicting direction: **West**

Lucky: Ceremony, Activating Feng Shui cures, Wedding, Dressmaking, Starting a construction, Setting up a bed/stove, Starting a business, Funeral.
Avoid: None.

---

8 (02/06)

Tuesday
Geng Shen (庚申) - Wood

Happiness star: **Northwest**, Wealth star: **East**
Conflicting sign: **Tiger**, Conflicting direction: **South**

Lucky: Ceremony, Removing Feng Shui cures, Bath, House cleaning, Hunting, Fishing, Funeral.
Avoid: Wedding, Setting up a bed, Starting a business, Moving to a new house.

---

9 (02/07)

Wednesday
Xin You (辛酉) - Wood

Happiness star: **Southwest**, Wealth star: **East**
Conflicting sign: **Rabbit**, Conflicting direction: **East**

Lucky: Demolition.
Avoid: Avoid any festive event.

---

10 (02/08)

Thursday
Ren Xu (壬戌) - Water

Happiness star: **South**, Wealth star: **South**
Conflicting sign: **Dragon**, Conflicting direction: **North**

Lucky: Travel, Wedding, Dressmaking, Starting a business, Setting up a bed, Funeral.
Avoid: Moving to a new house.

11 (02/09)

Friday
Kui Hai (癸亥) - Water

Happiness star: **Southeast**, Wealth star: **South**
Conflicting sign: **Snake,** Conflicting direction: **West**

Lucky: Ceremony, Signing a contract, Dressmaking, Starting a construction, Setting up a bed/ stove, Moving to a new house, Starting a business, Trading, Hunting, Planting, Visiting a doctor.
Avoid: Wedding, Activating Feng Shui cures, Funeral, Sharp knives.

12 (02/10)

Saturday
Jia Zi (甲子) - Metal

Happiness star: **Northeast**, Wealth star: **Southeast**
Conflicting sign: **Horse,** Conflicting direction: **South**

Lucky: Ceremony, Wedding, Bath, Haircut, Planting.
Avoid: Moving to a new house, Setting up a bed, Sharp knives.

13 (02/11)

Sunday
Yi Chou (乙丑) - Metal

Happiness star: **Northwest**, Wealth star: **Southeast**
Conflicting sign: **Goat,** Conflicting direction: **East**

Lucky: Ceremony, Travel, Adopting animals, Wedding, Dressmaking, Starting a construction, Visiting a doctor, Setting up a bed/stove.
Avoid: Moving to a new house, Activating Feng Shui cures, Starting a business, Funeral.

Weekly review/ gratitude:

March 2022

Week 12

March

S	M	T	W	T	F	S
27	28	1	2	3	4	5
6	7	8	9	10	11	12
13	14	15	16	17	18	19
20	21	22	23	24	25	26
27	28	29	30	31	1	2

---

14 (lunar date: 02/12)   **Monday**
Bing Yin (丙寅) - Fire

Happiness star: **Southwest**, Wealth star: **West**
Conflicting sign: **Monkey**, Conflicting direction: **North**

Lucky: Signing a contract, Trading, Dressmaking, Starting a construction, Setting up a bed, Funeral.
Avoid: None.

---

15 (02/13)   **Tuesday**
Ding Mao (丁卯) - Fire

Happiness star: **South**, Wealth star: **West**
Conflicting sign: **Rooster**, Conflicting direction: **West**

Lucky: Ceremony, Travel, Activating Feng Shui cures, Adopting animals, Dressmaking, Wedding, Moving to a new house, Starting a business, Visiting a doctor, Funeral.
Avoid: Starting a construction.

---

16 (02/14)   **Wednesday**
Wu Chen (戊辰) - Wood

Happiness star: **Southeast**, Wealth star: **North**
Conflicting sign: **Dog**, Conflicting direction: **South**

Lucky: Removing Feng Shui cures, Pest control.
Avoid: Any major festive event.

---

17 (02/15)   **Thursday**
Ji Si (己巳) - Wood

Happiness star: **Northeast**, Wealth star: **North**
Conflicting sign: **Pig**, Conflicting direction: **East**

Lucky: Ceremony, Haircut, Setting up a bed/stove, Starting a business, Trading, Adopting animals.
Avoid: Wedding, Moving to a new house, Starting a construction, Activating Feng Shui cures.

Weekly goals/ to do:

_____
_____
_____
_____
_____

18 (02/16)   **Friday**
                                          Geng Wu (庚午) - **Earth**
Happiness star: **Northwest**, Wealth star: **East**
Conflicting sign: **Rat,** Conflicting direction: **North**

Lucky: None.
Avoid: Any major festive event, avoid visiting sick patients.

19 (02/17)   Saturday
                                          Xin Wei (辛未) - **Earth**
Happiness star: **Southwest**, Wealth star: **East**
Conflicting sign: **Ox,** Conflicting direction: **West**

Lucky: Ceremony, Adopting animals.
Avoid: Any major festive event.

20 (02/18) * *Spring Equinox (Chun Fen 春分)*   Sunday
                                          Ren Shen (壬申) - **Metal**
Happiness star: **South**, Wealth star: **South**
Conflicting sign: **Tiger,** Conflicting direction: **South**

Lucky: Ceremony, Dressmaking, Starting a construction, Hunting, Fishing, Funeral.
Avoid: Starting a business, Wedding, Setting up a bed.

Weekly review/ gratitude:

_____
_____
_____
_____
_____

March 2022

Week 13

March

S	M	T	W	T	F	S
27	28	1	2	3	4	5
6	7	8	9	10	11	12
13	14	15	16	17	18	19
20	21	22	23	24	25	26
27	28	29	30	31	1	2

---

21 (lunar date: 02/19)　　　　　　　　　　　**Monday**
Kui You (癸酉) - Metal

Happiness star: **Southeast**, Wealth star: **South**

Conflicting sign: **Rabbit,** Conflicting direction: **East**

Lucky: Visiting a doctor, demolition.

Avoid: Any major festive event.

---

22 (02/20)　　　　　　　　　　　　　　　　**Tuesday**
Jia Xu (甲戌) - Fire

Happiness star: **Northeast,** Wealth star: **Southeast**

Conflicting sign: **Dragon,** Conflicting direction: **North**

Lucky: Ceremony, Travel, Dressmaking, Wedding, Starting a construction, Setting up a bed/stove, Moving to a new house, Starting a business, Planting, funeral.

Avoid: Setting up a door.

---

23 (02/21)　　　　　　　　　　　　　　**Wednesday**
Yi Hai (乙亥) - Fire

Happiness star: **Northwest,** Wealth star: **Southeast**

Conflicting sign: **Snake,** Conflicting direction: **West**

Lucky: Ceremony, Travel, Activating Feng Shui cures, Dressmaking, Starting a construction, Setting up a bed/stove, Moving to a new house, Starting a business.

Avoid: Setting up a door, funeral, sharp knives.

---

24 (02/22)　　　　　　　　　　　　　　**Thursday**
Bing Zi (丙子) - Water

Happiness star: **Southwest,** Wealth star: **West**

Conflicting sign: **Horse** Conflicting direction: **South**

Lucky: Wedding, Dressmaking, Setting up a bed.

Avoid: Moving to a new house, Setting up a door, Funeral, Sharp knives.

Weekly goals/ to do:

---

25 (02/23)   **Friday**
                                                   Ding Chou (丁丑) - Water
Happiness star: **South**, Wealth star: **West**
Conflicting sign: **Goat,** Conflicting direction: **East**

Lucky: Ceremony, Adopting animals, Dressmaking, Starting a construction, Setting up a bed/
stove, Moving to a new house.
Avoid: Activating Feng Shui cures, Wedding, Starting a business, Funeral.

---

26 (02/24)   **Saturday**
                                                   Wu Yin (戊寅) - Earth
Happiness star: **Southeast**, Wealth star: **North**
Conflicting sign: **Monkey,** Conflicting direction: **North**

Lucky: Adopting animals, Dressmaking, Starting a construction, Setting up a bed/stove, Funeral.
Avoid: Wedding, Moving to a new house.

---

27 (02/25)   **Sunday**
                                                   Ji Mao (己卯) - Earth
Happiness star: **Northeast**, Wealth star: **North**
Conflicting sign: **Rooster,** Conflicting direction: **West**

Lucky: Travel, Setting up a bed, Signing a contract, Starting a business.
Avoid: Starting a construction, Moving to a new house, Wedding, Funeral, Visiting sick patients.

Weekly review/ gratitude:

March - April

2022

Week 14

March

S	M	T	W	T	F	S
27	28	1	2	3	4	5
6	7	8	9	10	11	12
13	14	15	16	17	18	19
20	21	22	23	24	25	26
27	28	29	30	31	1	2

---

28 (lunar date: 02/26)

Monday

Geng Chen (庚辰) - Metal

Happiness star: **Northwest,** Wealth star: **East**

Conflicting sign: **Dog,** Conflicting direction: **South**

Lucky: Ceremony Travel, Removing Feng Shui cures, Bath, Haircut, House cleaning, Pest control.

Avoid: Any major festive event.

---

29 (02/27)

Tuesday

Xin Si (辛巳) - Metal

Happiness star: **Southwest,** Wealth star: **East**

Conflicting sign: **Pig,** Conflicting direction: **East**

Lucky: Ceremony, Haircut, Dressmaking, Meeting friends, Setting up a bed/stove/door, Starting a business, Trading.

Avoid: Wedding, Moving to a new house, Activating Feng Shui cures, Starting a construction.

---

30 (02/28)

Wednesday

Ren Wu (壬午) - Wood

Happiness star: **South,** Wealth star: **South**

Conflicting sign: **Rat,** Conflicting direction: **North**

Lucky: Ceremony, Wedding, Fixing a street/walkway, Starting a business.

Avoid: Setting up a stove, Moving to a new house, Funeral, Visiting sick patients.

---

31 (02/29)

Thursday

Kui Wei (癸未) - Wood

Happiness star: **Southeast,** Wealth star: **South**

Conflicting sign: **Ox,** Conflicting direction: **West**

Lucky: Ceremony, Travel, Activating Feng Shui cures, Wedding, Moving to a new house, Setting up a bed/stove, Starting a business, Funeral.

Avoid: None.

Apr 1 (03/01)   **Friday**
                                                    Jia Shen (甲申) - Water
Happiness star: **Northeast**, Wealth star: **Southeast**
Conflicting sign: **Tiger,** Conflicting direction: **South**

Lucky: Ceremony, Travel, Activating Feng Shui cures, Starting a construction, Moving to a new house, Funeral.
Avoid: Wedding, Starting a business, Setting up a bed/stove.

---

2 (03/02)   **Saturday**
                                                    Yi You (乙酉) - Water
Happiness star: **Northwest**, Wealth star: **Southeast**
Conflicting sign: **Rabbit** Conflicting direction: **East**

Lucky: Ceremony, Visiting a doctor, Demolition.
Avoid: Any major festive event.

---

3 (03/03)   **Sunday**
                                                    Bing Wu (丙戌) - Earth
Happiness star: **Southwest**, Wealth star: **West**
Conflicting sign: **Dragon,** Conflicting direction: **North**

Lucky: Ceremony, Travel, Dressmaking, Wedding, Starting a construction, Setting up a bed/door, Hunting, Fishing, Trading.
Avoid: Funeral.

Weekly review/ gratitude:

April 2022

Week 15

April

S	M	T	W	T	F	S
27	28	29	30	31	1	2
3	4	5	6	7	8	9
10	11	12	13	14	15	16
17	18	19	20	21	22	23
24	25	26	27	28	29	30

---

4 (lunar date: 03/04)   **Monday**
                                                    Ding Hai (丁亥) - Earth

Happiness star: **South**, Wealth star: **West**

Conflicting sign: **Snake**, Conflicting direction: **West**

Lucky: Ceremony, Activating Feng Shui cures, Dressmaking, Starting a construction, Visiting a doctor, Setting up a bed.

Avoid: Wedding, Sharp knives.

---

5 (03/05) *Clear and Bright (Qing Ming 清明)*   **Tuesday**
                                                    Wu Zi (戊子) - Fire

Happiness star: **Southeast**, Wealth star: **North**

Conflicting sign: **Horse,** Conflicting direction: **South**

Lucky: Ceremony, Activating Feng Shui cures, Dressmaking, Starting a construction, Starting a business, Setting up a bed/stove, Trading.

Avoid: Wedding, Moving to a new house, Sharp knives.

---

6 (03/06)   **Wednesday**
                                                    Ji Chou (己丑) - Fire

Happiness star: **Northeast**, Wealth star: **North**

Conflicting sign: **Goat,** Conflicting direction: **East**

Lucky: Ceremony, Fishing, Adopting animals, Pest control.

Avoid: Any major festive event.

---

7 (03/07)   **Thursday**
                                                    Geng Yin (庚寅) - Wood

Happiness star: **Northwest**, Wealth star: **East**

Conflicting sign: **Monkey,** Conflicting direction: **North**

Lucky: Travel, Starting a construction, Starting a business, Trading, Visiting a doctor, Planting.

Avoid: Wedding, Activating Feng Shui cures, Funeral, Moving to a new house.

---

8 (03/08)

Friday
Xin Mao (辛卯) - Wood

Happiness star: **Southwest**, Wealth star: **East**
Conflicting sign: **Rooster,** Conflicting direction: **West**

Lucky: Ceremony, Wedding, Dressmaking, Setting up a bed/stove, Funeral.
Avoid: Setting up a door.

---

9 (03/09)

Saturday
Ren Chen (壬辰) - Water

Happiness star: **South**, Wealth star: **South**
Conflicting sign: **Dog,** Conflicting direction: **South**

Lucky: Travel, Ceremony, Dressmaking, Starting a business, Trading, Setting up a bed.
Avoid: Startomg a construction, Wedding, Moving to a new house, Funeral.

---

10 (03/10)

Sunday
Kui Si (癸巳) - Water

Happiness star: **Southeast**, Wealth star: **South**
Conflicting sign: **Pig** Conflicting direction: **East**

Lucky: Wedding, Dressmaking, Adopting animals, Starting a construction, Moving to a new house, Meeting friends, Setting up a bed, House cleaning.
Avoid: Activating Feng Shui cures, Starting a business, Funeral.

Weekly review/ gratitude:

April 2022

Week 16

April

S	M	T	W	T	F	S
27	28	29	30	31	1	2
3	4	5	6	7	8	9
10	11	12	13	14	15	16
17	18	19	20	21	22	23
24	25	26	27	28	29	30

---

11 (lunar date: 03/11)   **Monday**

Jia Wu (甲午) - Metal

Happiness star: **Northeast**, Wealth star: **Southeast**

Conflicting sign: **Rat,** Conflicting direction: **North**

Lucky: Ceremony, Wedding, Haircut, Meeting friends, Starting a business, Setting up a bed, Funeral.

Avoid: Moving to a new house, Starting a construction, Setting up a door.

---

12 (03/12)   **Tuesday**

Yi Wei (乙未) - Metal

Happiness star: **Northwest**, Wealth star: **Northeast**

Conflicting sign: **Ox,** Conflicting direction: **West**

Lucky: Ceremony, Setting up a stove, Starting a business, Fixinig a street/walkway.

Avoid: Starting a construction, Setting up a bed, Wedding, Funeral.

---

13 (03/13)   **Wednesday**

Bing Shen (丙申) - Fire

Happiness star: **Southwest**, Wealth star: **West**

Conflicting sign: **Tiger,** Conflicting direction: **South**

Lucky: Ceremony, Activating Feng Shui cures, Adopting animals, Dressmaking, Starting a construction, Starting a business, Funeral.

Avoid: Wedding, Moving to a new house.

---

14 (03/14)   **Thursday**

Ding You (丁酉) - Fire

Happiness star: **South**, Wealth star: **West**

Conflicting sign: **Rabbit,** Conflicting direction: **East**

Lucky: Ceremony, Dressmaking, Wedding, Moving to a new house, Setting up a bed, Adopting animals, Funeral.

Avoid: Starting a construction, Starting a business, Activating Feng Shui cures.

Weekly goals/ to do:

---

15 (03/15) **Friday**
Wu Xu (戊戌) - Wood

Happiness star: **Southeast**, Wealth star: **North**
Conflicting sign: **Dragon,** Conflicting direction: **North**

Lucky: Ceremony, Removing Feng Shui cures, Bath, Visiting a doctor, demolition.
Avoid: Any major festive event.

---

16 (03/16) Saturday
Ji Hai (己亥) - Wood

Happiness star: **Northeast**, Wealth star: **North**
Conflicting sign: **Snake**, Conflicting direction: **West**

Lucky: Bath, Fishing.
Avoid: Any major festive event, Sharp knives.

---

17 (03/17) Sunday
Geng Zi (庚子) - Earth

Happiness star: **Northeast**, Wealth star: **East**
Conflicting sign: **Horse**, Conflicting direction: **South**

Lucky: Ceremony, Activating Feng Shui cures, Travel, Trading, Starting a business, Setting up a bed, dressmaking.
Avoid: Moving to a new house, Wedding, Funeral, Sharp knives.

Weekly review/ gratitude:

April 2022

Week 17

April

S	M	T	W	T	F	S
27	28	29	30	31	1	2
3	4	5	6	7	8	9
10	11	12	13	14	15	16
17	18	19	20	21	22	23
24	25	26	27	28	29	30

---

18 (lunar date: 03/18)

Happiness star: **Southwest**, Wealth star: **East**

Conflicting sign: **Goat**, Conflicting direction: **East**

Monday
Xin Chou (辛丑) - Earth

Lucky: Ceremony, Fishing, Adopting animals.

Avoid: Any major festive event.

---

19 (03/19)

Happiness star: **South**, Wealth star: **South**

Conflicting sign: **Monkey**, Conflicting direction: **North**

Tuesday
Ren Yin (壬寅) - Metal

Lucky: Travel, Activating Feng Shui cures, Wedding, Dressmaking, Moving to a new house, Setting up a bed, Visiting a doctor, Meeting friends, Planting, Adopting animals.
Avoid: Visiting sick patients, Starting a business.

---

20 (03/20) *Grain Rain (Gu Yu 穀雨)*

Happiness star: **Southeast**, Wealth star: **South**

Conflicting sign: **Rooster**, Conflicting direction: **West**

Wednesday
Kui Mao (癸卯) - Metal

Lucky: Travel, Wedding, Dressmaking, Setting up a bed/stove, Trading, Pest control, Funeral.
Avoid: None.

---

21 (03/21)

Happiness star: **Northeast**, Wealth star: **Southeast**

Conflicting sign: **Dog**, Conflicting direction: **South**

Thursday
Jia Chen (甲辰) - Fire

Lucky: Travel, Starting a business, Fixing animal houses.
Avoid: Starting a construction, Wedding, Funeral.

---

22 (03/22)

Happiness star: **Northwest**, Wealth star: **Southeast**

Conflicting sign: **Pig,** Conflicting direction: **East**

Friday
Yi Si (乙巳) - Fire

Lucky: Ceremony, Wedding, Moving to a new house, Setting up a bed, Visiting a doctor, Dressmaking, Fixing animal houses.

Avoid: Activating Feng Shui cures, Starting a business, Funeral.

---

23 (03/23)

Happiness star: **Southwest**, Wealth star: **West**

Conflicting sign: **Monkey,** Conflicting direction: **North**

Saturday
Bing Wu (丙午) - Water

Lucky: Starting a business, Ceremony, Haircut, Meeting friends, Adopting animals, Setting up a bed, Funeral.

Avoid: Wedding, Activating Feng Shui cures, Moving to a new house.

---

24 (03/24)

Happiness star: **South**, Wealth star: **West**

Conflicting sign: **Ox,** Conflicting direction: **West**

Sunday
Ding Wei (丁未) - Water

Lucky: Ceremony, Fixing a street/walkway, Funeral.

Avoid: Wedding, Moving to a new house, Setting up a bed/stove.

Weekly review/ gratitude:

April - May 2022

Week 18

April

S	M	T	W	T	F	S
27	28	29	30	31	1	2
3	4	5	6	7	8	9
10	11	12	13	14	15	16
17	18	19	20	21	22	23
24	25	26	27	28	29	30

---

25 (lunar date: 03/25)   **Monday**
                                                      Wu Shen (戊申) - Earth

Happiness star: **Southeast**, Wealth star: **North**

Conflicting sign: **Tiger**, Conflicting direction: **South**

Lucky: Ceremony, Adopting animals, Activating Feng Shui cures, Removing Feng Shui items, Bath, Starting a business, Trading, Pest control, House cleaning.
Avoid: Wedding, Moving to a new house, Funeral.

---

26 (03/26)   **Tuesday**
                                                       Ji You (己酉) - Earth

Happiness star: **Northeast**, Wealth star: **North**

Conflicting sign: **Rabbit**, Conflicting direction: **East**

Lucky: Ceremony, Renovation, Dressmaking, Moving to a new house, Setting up a bed/stove, Adopting animals, funeral, Visiting a doctor.
Avoid: Activating Feng Shui cures, Wedding, Starting a construction.

---

27 (03/27)   **Wednesday**
                                                       Geng Xu (庚戌) - Metal

Happiness star: **Northwest**, Wealth star: **East**

Conflicting sign: **Dragon**, Conflicting direction: **North**

Lucky: Ceremony, Removing Feng Shui items, Bath, Haircut, Visiting a doctor, Demolition.
Avoid: Any major festive event.

---

28 (03/28)   **Thursday**
                                                       Xin Hai (辛亥) - Metal

Happiness star: **Southwest**, Wealth star: **East**

Conflicting sign: **Snake**, Conflicting direction: **West**

Lucky: Bath, Meeting friends, House cleaning, Planting.
Avoid: Any major festive event, sharp knives.

Weekly goals/ to do:

---

29 (03/29)   **Friday**
                                                                                   Ren Zi (壬子) - Wood
Happiness star: **South**, Wealth star: **South**
Conflicting sign: **Horse,** Conflicting direction: **South**

Lucky: Ceremony, Activating Feng Shui cures, Dressmaking, Setting up a bed, Visiting a doctor,
Funeral, Starting a construction, Planting.
Avoid: Wedding, Moving to a new house, Sharp knives.

---

30 (03/30)   Saturday
                                                                                  Kui Chou (癸丑) - Wood
Happiness star: **Southeast**, Wealth star: **South**
Conflicting sign: **Goat,** Conflicting direction: **East**

Lucky: Ceremony, Hunting, Fishing.
Avoid: Any major festive event.

May 1 (04/01)   Sunday
                                                                                  Jia Yin (甲寅) - Water
Happiness star: **Northeast**, Wealth star: **Southeast**
Conflicting sign: **Monkey,** Conflicting direction: **North**

Lucky: Travel, Signing a contract, Dressmaking, Renovation, Setting up a bed/stove, Moving to a
new house, Starting a business, Trading, Planting.
Avoid: Visiting sick patients.

Weekly review/ gratitude:

May 2022

Week 19

May

S	M	T	W	T	F	S
1	2	3	4	5	6	7
8	9	10	11	12	13	14
15	16	17	18	19	20	21
22	23	24	25	26	27	28
29	30	31	1	2	3	4

---

2 (lunar date: 04/02)   **Monday**
Yi Mao (乙卯) - Water

Happiness star: **Northwest**, Wealth star: **Southeast**
Conflicting sign: **Rooster**, Conflicting direction: **West**

Lucky: Ceremony, Wedding, Dressmaking, Setting up a bed/stove, Funeral.
Avoid: Visiting sick patients, Starting a business, Setting up a door.

---

3 (04/03)   **Tuesday**
Bing Chen (丙辰) - Earth

Happiness star: **Southwest**, Wealth star: **West**
Conflicting sign: **Dog**, Conflicting direction: **South**

Lucky: Travel, Training animals, House cleaning.
Avoid: Activating Feng Shui cures, Starting a construction, Wedding,

---

4 (04/04)   **Wednesday**
Ding Si (丁巳) - Earth

Happiness star: **South**, Wealth star: **West**
Conflicting sign: **Pig**, Conflicting direction: **East**

Lucky: Ceremony, Activating Feng Shui cures, Trading, Planting, Adopting animals, Visiting a doctor.
Avoid: Funeral, Travel, Moving to a new house.

---

5 (04/05) * *Start of Summer (Li Xia 立夏)*   **Thursday**
Wu Wu (戊午) - Fire

Happiness star: **Southeast**, Wealth star: **North**
Conflicting sign: **Rat**, Conflicting direction: **North**

Lucky: Ceremony, Activating Feng Shui cures, Bath, Haircut, Trading, Pest control, Dressmaking, Planting.
Avoid: Starting a construction, Wedding, Travel.

Weekly goals/ to do:

---

6 (04/06)   **Friday**

Ji Wei (己未) - Fire

Happiness star: **Northeast**, Wealth star: **North**

Conflicting sign: **Ox,** Conflicting direction: **West**

Lucky: Ceremony, Pest control.

Avoid: Starting a business, Starting a construction, Wedding, Moving to a new house.

---

7 (04/07)   Saturday

Geng Shen (庚申) - Wood

Happiness star: **Northwest**, Wealth star: **East**

Conflicting sign: **Tiger,** Conflicting direction: **South**

Lucky: Ceremony, Travel, Dressmaking, Funeral, Trading, Starting a business, Planting.

Avoid: Setting up a bed, Wedding, Moving to anew house.

---

8 (04/08)   Sunday

Xin You (辛酉) - Wood

Happiness star: **Southwest**, Wealth star: **East**

Conflicting sign: **Rabbit,** Conflicting direction: **East**

Lucky: Ceremony, Travel, Activating Feng Shui cures, Wedding, Starting a construction, Starting a business, Funeral, Moving to a new house, Trading.

Avoid: None.

Weekly review/ gratitude:

May 2022

Week 20

May

S	M	T	W	T	F	S
1	2	3	4	5	6	7
8	9	10	11	12	13	14
15	16	17	18	19	20	21
22	23	24	25	26	27	28
29	30	31	1	2	3	4

---

9 (lunar date: 04/09)   **Monday**

Ren Xu (壬戌) - Water

Happiness star: **South**, Wealth star: **South**

Conflicting sign: **Dragon**, Conflicting direction: **North**

Lucky: Starting a construction, Moving to a new house, Setting up a bed, Funeral, Bath, Haircut, Meeting friends, Hunting.

Avoid: Activating Feng Shui cures, Wedding, Starting a business.

---

10 (04/10)   **Tuesday**

Kui Hai (癸亥) - Water

Happiness star: **Southwest**, Wealth star: **South**

Conflicting sign: **Snake,** Conflicting direction: **West**

Lucky: Demolition.

Avoid: Any major festive event.

---

11 (04/11)   **Wednesday**

Jia Zi (甲子) - Metal

Happiness star: **Northeast**, Wealth star: **Southeast**

Conflicting sign: **Horse,** Conflicting direction: **South**

Lucky: Ceremony, Travel, Adopting animals, Wedding, Starting a construction, Moving to a new house, Setting up a bed/stove, Starting a business, Funeral.

Avoid: Activating Feng Shui cures.

---

12 (04/12)   **Thursday**

Yi Chou (乙丑) - Metal

Happiness star: **Northwest**, Wealth star: **Southeast**

Conflicting sign: **Goat,** Conflicting direction: **East**

Lucky: Ceremony, Activating Feng Shui cures, Travel, Starting a construction, Setting up a bed/stove, Starting a business, Trading, Funeral.

Avoid: Wedding.

_____
_____
_____
_____

13 (04/13)   **Friday**
Happiness star: **Southwest**, Wealth star: **West**   Bing Yin (丙寅) - Fire
Conflicting sign: **Monkey,** Conflicting direction: **North**

Lucky: Travel, Signing a contract, Wedding, Dressmaking, Moving to a new house, Setting up a
bed, Meeting friends.
Avoid: Starting a construction, Funeral.

14 (04/14)   Saturday
Happiness star: **South**, Wealth star: **West**   Ding Mao (丁卯) - Fire
Conflicting sign: **Rooster,** Conflicting direction: **West**

Lucky: Ceremony, Activating Feng Shui cures, Wedding, Dressmaking, Starting a construction,
Setting up a bed, Starting a business, Visiting a doctor, Signing a contract.
Avoid: Moving to a new house, Travel, Funeral.

15 (04/15)   Sunday
Happiness star: **Southeast**, Wealth star: **North**   Wu Chen (戊辰) - Wood
Conflicting sign: **Dog,** Conflicting direction: **South**

Lucky: Ceremony, Travel, Starting a construction, Moving to a new house, Setting up a bed/
stove, Dressmaking, Trading, Pest control.
Avoid: Wedding, Activating Feng Shui cures.

Weekly review/ gratitude:

_____
_____
_____
_____

May 2022

Week 21

May

S	M	T	W	T	F	S
1	2	3	4	5	6	7
8	9	10	11	12	13	14
15	16	17	18	19	20	21
22	23	24	25	26	27	28
29	30	31	1	2	3	4

---

16 (lunar date: 04/16)

Monday

Ji Si (己巳) - Wood

Happiness star: **Northeast**, Wealth star: **North**

Conflicting sign: **Pig,** Conflicting direction: **East**

Lucky: Pest control.

Avoid: Any major festive event.

---

17 (04/17)

Tuesday

Geng Wu (庚午) - Earth

Happiness star: **Northwest**, Wealth star: **East**

Conflicting sign: **Rat,** Conflicting direction: **North**

Lucky: Ceremony, Travel, Adopting animals, Dressmaking, Starting a construction, Starting a business, Visiting a doctor, Planting.

Avoid: Visiting sick patients, Wedding, Activating Feng Shui cures.

---

18 (04/18)

Wednesday

Xin Wei (辛未) - Earth

Happiness star: **Southwest**, Wealth star: **East**

Conflicting sign: **Ox,** Conflicting direction: **West**

Lucky: Activating Feng Shui cures, Bath, Signing a contract, Wedding, Dressmaking, Setting up a bed/stove, Fixing a street/walkway, House cleaning, Fixing animal houses.

Avoid: Starting a construction, Starting a business, Funeral.

---

19 (04/19)

Thursday

Ren Shen (壬申) - Metal

Happiness star: **South**, Wealth star: **South**

Conflicting sign: **Tiger** Conflicting direction: **South**

Lucky: Ceremony, Bath, House cleaning, Fixing a street/walkway, Funeral.

Avoid: Wedding, Setting up a bed/stove, Activating Feng Shui cures.

---

20 (04/20)   **Friday**
                                           Kui You (癸酉) - Metal

Happiness star: **Southeast**, Wealth star: **South**
Conflicting sign: **Rabbit**, Conflicting direction: **East**

Lucky: Ceremony, Travel, Wedding, Starting a construction, Moving to a new house, Setting up a stove, Starting a business, Funeral.
Avoid: Adopting animals.

---

21 (04/21) * *Small (Grain) Full (Xiao Man 小满)*   Saturday
                                          Jia Xu (甲戌) - Fire

Happiness star: **Northeast**, Wealth star: **Southeast**
Conflicting sign: **Dragon**, Conflicting direction: **North**

Lucky: Ceremony, Activating Feng Shui cures, Travel, Bath, Haircut, Signing a contract, Wedding, Meeting friends, Fishing Hunting, Funeral, Visiting a doctor.
Avoid: Moving to a new house.

---

22 (04/22)   Sunday
                                          Yi Hai (乙亥) - Fire

Happiness star: **Northwest**, Wealth star: **Southeast**
Conflicting sign: **Snake**, Conflicting direction: **West**

Lucky: Ceremony, Removing Feng Shui cures, demolition.
Avoid: Any major festive event.

Weekly review/ gratitude:

May 2022

Week 22

May

S	M	T	W	T	F	S
1	2	3	4	5	6	7
8	9	10	11	12	13	14
15	16	17	18	19	20	21
22	23	24	25	26	27	28
29	30	31	1	2	3	4

---

23 (lunar date: 04/23)　　　　　　　　　　　　　　**Monday**

Bing Zi (丙子) - Water

Happiness star: **Southwest**, Wealth star: **West**

Conflicting sign: **Horse**, Conflicting direction: **South**

Lucky: Ceremony, Starting a construction, Moving to a new house, Setting up a bed, Dressmaking, Adopting animals, Starting a business, Trading, Planting.
Avoid: Wedding, Activating Feng Shui cures.

---

24 (04/24)　　　　　　　　　　　　　　　　**Tuesday**

Ding Chou (丁丑) - Water

Happiness star: **South**, Wealth star: **West**

Conflicting sign: **Goat,** Conflicting direction: **East**

Lucky: Ceremony, Activating Feng Shui cures, Adopting animals, Starting a construction, Starting a business, Setting up a bed, Visiting a doctor, Funeral.
Avoid: Wedding, Moving to a new house.

---

25 (04/25)　　　　　　　　　　　　　　**Wednesday**

Wu Yin (戊寅) - Earth

Happiness star: **Southeast**, Wealth star: **North**

Conflicting sign: **Monkey,** Conflicting direction: **North**

Lucky: Fishing, Hunting, Pest control.
Avoid: Sharp knives, starting a construction, Starting a business, Wedding, Moving to a new house, Funeral.

---

26 (04/26)　　　　　　　　　　　　　　**Thursday**

Ji Mao (己卯) - Earth

Happiness star: **Northeast**, Wealth star: **North**

Conflicting sign: **Rooster,** Conflicting direction: **West**

Lucky: Visiting a doctor, Activating Feng Shui cures, Travel, Signing a contract, Wedding, Dressmaking, Meeting friends, Setting up a bed, Funeral.
Avoid: Sharp knives, Moving to a new house.

Weekly goals/ to do:

---

27 (04/27)

Friday
Geng Chen (庚辰) - Metal

Happiness star: **Northwest**, Wealth star: **East**
Conflicting sign: **Dog,** Conflicting direction: **South**

Lucky: Ceremony, Travel, Wedding, Starting a construction, Setting up a bed/stove, Funeral.
Avoid: Moving to a new house, Activating Feng Shui cures.

---

28 (04/28)

Saturday
Xin Si (辛巳) - Metal

Happiness star: **Southwest**, Wealth star: **East**
Conflicting sign: **Pig,** Conflicting direction: **East**

Lucky: Ceremony, Removing Feng Shui items, Pest control.
Avoid: Any major festive event.

---

29 (04/29)

Sunday
Ren Wu (壬午) - Wood

Happiness star: **South**, Wealth star: **South**
Conflicting sign: **Rat,** Conflicting direction: **North**

Lucky: Ceremony, Travel, Adopting animals, Wedding, Starting a construction, Moving to a new house, Starting a business, Funeral.
Avoid: Setting up a bed.

Weekly review/ gratitude:

May - June 2022

Week 23

June

S	M	T	W	T	F	S
29	30	31	1	2	3	4
5	6	7	8	9	10	11
12	13	14	15	16	17	18
19	20	21	22	23	24	25
26	27	28	29	30	1	2

---

30 (lunar date: 05/01)   **Monday**

Happiness star: **Southeast**, Wealth star: **South**   Kui Wei (癸未) - Wood

Conflicting sign: **Ox,** Conflicting direction: **West**

Lucky: Ceremony, Meeting friends, Pest control.

Avoid: Moving to a new house, Starting a construction, Wedding, Funeral.

---

31 (05/02)   **Tuesday**

Happiness star: **Northeast**, Wealth star: **Southeast**   Jia Shen (甲申) - Water

Conflicting sign: **Tiger,** Conflicting direction: **South**

Lucky: Ceremony, Bath, Wedding, Dressmaking, House cleaning, Fixing a street/walkway, Funeral.

Avoid: Setting up a bed, Activating Feng Shui cures.

Jun 1 (05/03)   **Wednesday**

Happiness star: **Northwest**, Wealth star: **Southeast**   Yi You (乙酉) - Water

Conflicting sign: **Rabbit,** Conflicting direction: **East**

Lucky: Ceremony, Activating Feng Shui cures, Wedding, Travel, Starting a construction, Moving to a new house, Setting up a bed/stove, Adopting animals, Funeral.

Avoid: None.

---

2 (05/04)   **Thursday**

Happiness star: **Southwest**, Wealth star: **West**   Bing Xu (丙戌) - Earth

Conflicting sign: **Dragon,** Conflicting direction: **North**

Lucky: Ceremony, Activating Feng Shui cures, Wedding, Dressmaking, Starting a construction, Moving to a new house, Setting up a bed/door, Signing a contract.

Avoid: Funeral.

3 (05/05) ** Dragon Boat Festival*   **Friday**
Happiness star: **South**, Wealth star: **West**   Ding Hai (丁亥) - Earth
Conflicting sign: **Snake**, Conflicting direction: **West**

Lucky: Demolition, Bath.
Avoid: Any major festive event.

4 (05/06)   **Saturday**
Happiness star: **Southeast**, Wealth star: **North**   Wu Zi (戊子) - Fire
Conflicting sign: **Horse**, Conflicting direction: **South**

Lucky: Ceremony, Travel, Adopting animals, Wedding, Starting a construction, Setting up a bed/ stove, Moving to a new house, Funeral.
Avoid: Starting a business, Activating Feng Shui cures.

5 (05/07)   **Sunday**
Happiness star: **Northeast**, Wealth star: **North**   Ji Chou (己丑) - Fire
Conflicting sign: **Goat**, Conflicting direction: **East**

Lucky: Ceremony, Travel, Starting a construction, Setting up a bed/stove, Starting a business, Planting, Adopting animals, Funeral.
Avoid: Wedding, Moving to a new house, Activating Feng Shui cures.

Weekly review/ gratitude:

June 2022

Week 24

June

S	M	T	W	T	F	S
29	30	31	1	2	3	4
5	6	7	8	9	10	11
12	13	14	15	16	17	18
19	20	21	22	23	24	25
26	27	28	29	30	1	2

---

6 (lunar date: 05/08) * *Planting Grains (Man Zhong 芒种)*

Monday

Geng Yin (庚寅) - Wood

Happiness star: **Northwest,** Wealth star: **East**

Conflicting sign: **Monkey,** Conflicting direction: **North**

Lucky: Activating Feng Shui cures, Starting a construction, Setting up a bed/stove, Starting a business, Visiting a doctor, Travel, Planting, Funeral.

Avoid: Sharp knives, Wedding, Moving to a new house.

---

7 (05/09)

Tuesday

Xin Mao (辛卯) - Wood

Happiness star: **Southwest,** Wealth star: **East**

Conflicting sign: **Rooster,** Conflicting direction: **West**

Lucky: Ceremony, Hunting, Fishing.

Avoid: Sharp knives, **Any major festive event.**

---

8 (05/10)

Wednesday

Ren Chen (壬辰) - Water

Happiness star: **South,** Wealth star: **South**

Conflicting sign: **Dog,** Conflicting direction: **South**

Lucky: Ceremony, Travel, Dressmaking, Wedding, Starting a construction, Setting up a bed/stove, Moving to a new house, Visiting a doctor.

Avoid: Activating Feng Shui cures.

---

9 (05/11)

Thursday

Kui Si (癸巳) - Water

Happiness star: **Southeast,** Wealth star: **South**

Conflicting sign: **Pig,** Conflicting direction: **East**

Lucky: Dressmaking, Wedding, Setting up a stove/door, Moving to a new house, Pest control, Adopting animals.

Avoid: Starting a business.

---

10 (05/12)

Happiness star: **Northeast,** Wealth star: **Southeast**

Conflicting sign: **Rat,** Conflicting direction: **North**

Friday

Jia Wu (甲午) - Metal

Lucky: Ceremony, Funeral.

Avoid: Starting a construction, Wedding, Moving to a new house.

---

11 (05/13)

Happiness star: **Northwest,** Wealth star: **Southeast**

Conflicting sign: **Ox,** Conflicting direction: **West**

Saturday

Yi Wei (乙未) - Metal

Lucky: Ceremony, Travel, Activating Feng Shui cures, Wedding, Dressmaking, Moving to a new house, Setting up a bed, Starting a business.

Avoid: None.

---

12 (05/14)

Happiness star: **Southwest,** Wealth star: **West**

Conflicting sign: **Tiger,** Conflicting direction: **South**

Sunday

Bing Shen (丙申) - Fire

Lucky: Ceremony, Wedding, Dressmaking, Moving to a new house, Setting up a door, Planting, Adopting animals, Visiting a doctor, Funeral.

Avoid: Starting a construction, Activating Feng Shui cures.

Weekly review/ gratitude:

June 2022

Week 25

June

S	M	T	W	T	F	S
29	30	31	1	2	3	4
5	6	7	8	9	10	11
12	13	14	15	16	17	18
19	20	21	22	23	24	25
26	27	28	29	30	1	2

---

13 (lunar date: 05/15)　　　　　　　　　　　　　**Monday**

Ding You (丁酉) - Fire

Happiness star: **South**, Wealth star: **West**

Conflicting sign: **Rabbit**, Conflicting direction: **East**

Lucky: Ceremony, Bath, Fixing a street/walkway, House cleaning,

Avoid: Wedding, Moving to a new house, Funeral, Activating Feng Shui cures.

---

14 (05/16)　　　　　　　　　　　　　　　　**Tuesday**

Wu Xu (戊戌) - Wood

Happiness star: **Southeast**, Wealth star: **North**

Conflicting sign: **Dragon**, Conflicting direction: **North**

Lucky: Ceremony, Travel, Wedding, Starting a construction, Moving to a new house, Setting up a bed, Starting a business, Trading, Adopting animals, Funeral.

Avoid: None.

---

15 (05/17)　　　　　　　　　　　　　**Wednesday**

Ji Hai (己亥) - Wood

Happiness star: **Northeast**, Wealth star: **North**

Conflicting sign: **Snake**, Conflicting direction: **West**

Lucky: Ceremony, Travel, Activating Feng Shui cures, Dressmaking, Starting a construction, Moving to a new house, Setting up a bed, Visiting a doctor, Bath, Planting.

Avoid: Wedding, Funeral.

---

16 (05/18)　　　　　　　　　　　　　　**Thursday**

Geng Zi (庚子) - Earth

Happiness star: **Northwest**, Wealth star: **East**

Conflicting sign: **Horse**, Conflicting direction: **South**

Lucky: Demolition.

Avoid: Any major festive event.

Weekly goals/ to do:

_____
_____
_____
_____

---

17 (05/19)   **Friday**
                                              Xin Chou (辛丑) - Earth

Happiness star: **Southwest**, Wealth star: **East**
Conflicting sign: **Goat**, Conflicting direction: **East**

Lucky: Ceremony, Activating Feng Shui cures, Wedding, Dressmaking, Starting a construction, Setting up a bed, Funeral.
Avoid: Moving to a new house.

---

18 (05/20)   **Saturday**
                                                Ren Yin (壬寅) - Metal

Happiness star: **South**, Wealth star: **South**
Conflicting sign: **Monkey**, Conflicting direction: **North**

Lucky: Activating Feng Shui cures, Dressmaking, Starting a construction, Setting up a bed/door, Starting a business, Trading, Visiting a doctor, Funeral.
Avoid: Wedding, Moving to a new house, Sharp knives.

---

19 (05/21)   Sunday
                                                Kui Mao (癸卯) - Metal

Happiness star: **Southeast**, Wealth star: **South**
Conflicting sign: **Rooster**, Conflicting direction: **West**

Lucky: Ceremony, Setting up a stove, Planting.
Avoid: Wedding, Starting a business, Moving to a new house, Funeral, Sharp knives.

Weekly review/ gratitude:

_____
_____
_____
_____

June 2022

Week 26

June

S	M	T	W	T	F	S
29	30	31	1	2	3	4
5	6	7	8	9	10	11
12	13	14	15	16	17	18
19	20	21	22	23	24	25
26	27	28	29	30	1	2

---

20 (lunar date: 05/22)   **Monday**
Jia Chen (甲辰) - Fire

Happiness star: **Northeast,** Wealth star: **Southeast**

Conflicting sign: **Dog,** Conflicting direction: **South**

Lucky: Ceremony, Visiting a doctor, Setting up a stove, Planting.

Avoid: Any major festive event.

---

21 (05/23) * *Summer Solstice (Xia Zhi 夏至)*   **Tuesday**
Yi Si (乙巳) - Fire

Happiness star: **Northwest,** Wealth star: **Southeast**

Conflicting sign: **Pig,** Conflicting direction: **East**

Lucky: Dressmaking, Adopting animals, Starting a construction, Setting up a stove, Pest control, Fixing animal houses.

Avoid: Wedding, Moving to a new house, Activating Feng Shui cures, Funeral.

---

22 (05/24)   **Wednesday**
Bing Wu (丙午) - Water

Happiness star: **Southwest,** Wealth star: **West**

Conflicting sign: **Rat,** Conflicting direction: **North**

Lucky: Ceremony, Funeral.

Avoid: Starting a construction, Wedding, Setting up a bed, Moving to a new house.

---

23 (05/25)   **Thursday**
Ding Wei (丁未) - Water

Happiness star: **South,** Wealth star: **West**

Conflicting sign: **Ox,** Conflicting direction: **West**

Lucky: Ceremony, Travel, Activating Feng Shui cures, Starting a construction, Setting up a bed, Hunting, Planting, Fixing animal houses.

Avoid: Wedding, Moving to a new house, Starting a business, Funeral.

24 (05/26)

Friday
Wu Shen (戊申) - Earth

Happiness star: **Southeast**, Wealth star: **North**
Conflicting sign: **Tiger**, Conflicting direction: **South**

Lucky: Ceremony, Travel, Dressmaking, Starting a business, Visiting a doctor, Funeral, Planting.
Avoid: Wedding, Activating Feng Shui cures, Moving to a new house, Signing a contract.

25 (05/27)

Saturday
Ji You (己酉) - Earth

Happiness star: **Northeast**, Wealth star: **North**
Conflicting sign: **Rabbit**, Conflicting direction: **East**

Lucky: Ceremony, Bath, Haircut, Fixing a street/walkway, House cleaning.
Avoid: Wedding, Moving to a new house, Travel, Starting a business, Funeral.

26 (05/28)

Sunday
Geng Xu (庚戌) - Metal

Happiness star: **Northwest**, Wealth star: **East**
Conflicting sign: **Dragon**, Conflicting direction: **North**

Lucky: Ceremony, Activating Feng Shui cures, Travel, Wedding, Starting a construction, Moving to a new house, Setting up a bed, Adopting animals, Funeral.
Avoid: None.

Weekly review/ gratitude:

June - July 2022

Week 27

June

S	M	T	W	T	F	S
29	30	31	1	2	3	4
5	6	7	8	9	10	11
12	13	14	15	16	17	18
19	20	21	22	23	24	25
26	27	28	29	30	1	2

---

27 (lunar date: 05/29)

Monday
Xin Hai (辛亥) - Metal

Happiness star: **Southwest**, Wealth star: **East**
Conflicting sign: **Snake**, Conflicting direction: **West**

Lucky: Ceremony, Activating Feng Shui cures, Bath, Dressmaking, Meeting friends, Starting a construction, Setting up a door/bed/stove, Moving to a new house.
Avoid: Funeral.

---

28 (05/30)

Tuesday
Ren Zi (壬子) - Wood

Happiness star: **South**, Wealth star: **South**
Conflicting sign: **Horse**, Conflicting direction: **South**

Lucky: Demolition.
Avoid: Any major festive event.

---

29 (06/01)

Wednesday
Kui Chou (癸丑) - Wood

Happiness star: **Southeast**, Wealth star: **South**
Conflicting sign: **Goat**, Conflicting direction: **East**

Lucky: Ceremony, Starting a construction, Setting up a bed, Trading, Starting a business.
Avoid: Wedding, Moving to a new house, Funeral.

---

30 (06/02)

Thursday
Jia Yin (甲寅) - Water

Happiness star: **Northeast**, Wealth star: **Southeast**
Conflicting sign: **Monkey**, Conflicting direction: **North**

Lucky: Travel, Dressmaking, Starting a construction, Setting up a bed/stove, Starting a business, Visiting a doctor, Funeral, Planting.
Avoid: Sharp knives, Wedding, Moving to a new house, Activating Feng Shui cures.

Weekly goals/ to do:

_____
_____
_____
_____

Jul 1 (06/03)   **Friday**
                                              Yi Mao (乙卯) - Water
Happiness star: **Northwest**, Wealth star: **Southeast**
Conflicting sign: **Rooster**, Conflicting direction: **West**

Lucky: Ceremony, Setting up a stove.
Avoid: Sharp knives, Visiting sick patients, Moving to a new house, Wedding, Funeral.

2 (06/04)   Saturday
                                              Bing Chen (丙辰) - Earth
Happiness star: **Southwest**, Wealth star: **West**
Conflicting sign: **Dog**, Conflicting direction: **South**

Lucky: Ceremony, Travel, Activating Feng Shui cures, Adopting animals, Wedding, Starting a construction, Setting up a bed, Moving to a new house, Visiting a doctor.
Avoid: Setting up a stove.

3 (06/05)   Sunday
                                              Ding Si (丁巳) - Earth
Happiness star: **South**, Wealth star: **West**
Conflicting sign: **Pig**, Conflicting direction: **East**

Lucky: Dressmaking, Wedding, Starting a construction, Moving to a new house, Setting up a door, Pest control, Fixing animal houses.
Avoid: Funeral.

Weekly review/ gratitude:

_____
_____
_____
_____

July 2022

Week 28

	S	M	T	W	T	F	S
July							
	26	27	28	29	30	1	2
	3	4	5	6	7	8	9
	10	11	12	13	14	15	16
	17	18	19	20	21	22	23
	24	25	26	27	28	29	30
	31	1	2	3	4	5	6

---

4 (lunar date: 06/06)   **Monday**

Wu Wu (戊午) - Fire

Happiness star: **Southeast**, Wealth star: **North**

Conflicting sign: **Rat,** Conflicting direction: **North**

Lucky: Ceremony, Pest control, Training animals.

Avoid: Moving to a new house, Starting a construction, Activating Feng Shui cures, Wedding, Starting a business.

---

5 (06/07)   **Tuesday**

Ji Wei (己未) - Fire

Happiness star: **Northeast**, Wealth star: **North**

Conflicting sign: **Ox,** Conflicting direction: **West**

Lucky: Ceremony, Travel, Adopting animals, Dressmaking, Starting a construction, Setting up a bed, Moving to a new house, Starting a business, Trading, Planting.

Avoid: Wedding, Activating Feng Shui cures, Funeral.

---

6 (06/08)   **Wednesday**

Geng Shen (庚申) - Wood

Happiness star: **Northwest**, Wealth star: **East**

Conflicting sign: **Tiger,** Conflicting direction: **South**

Lucky: Ceremony, Travel, Activating Feng Shui cures, Wedding, Dressmaking, Moving to a new house, Starting a business, Funeral.

Avoid: Starting a construction.

---

7 (06/09) * *Lesser Heat (Xiao Shu 小暑)*   **Thursday**

Xin You (辛酉) - Wood

Happiness star: **Southwest**, Wealth star: **East**

Conflicting sign: **Rabbit,** Conflicting direction: **East**

Lucky: Travel, Starting a business, Dressmaking, Ceremony, Setting up a bed, Funeral.

Avoid: Wedding, Moving to a new house.

---

8 (06/10)   **Friday**
Happiness star: **South**, Wealth star: **South**   Ren Xu (壬戌) - Water
Conflicting sign: **Dragon,** Conflicting direction: **North**

Lucky: Wedding, Funeral, Fishing , Hunting.
Avoid: Starting a construction, Activating Feng Shui cures, Setting up a door/stove.

---

9 (06/11)   Saturday
Happiness star: **Southeast**, Wealth star: **South**   Kui Hai (癸亥) - Water
Conflicting sign: **Snake,** Conflicting direction: **West**

Lucky: Ceremony, Bath.
Avoid: Wedding, Moving to a new house, Setting up a stove, Funeral.

---

10 (06/12)   Sunday
Happiness star: **Northeast**, Wealth star: **Southeast** Jia Zi (甲子) - Metal
Conflicting sign: **Horse,** Conflicting direction: **South**

Lucky: Dressmaking, Travel, Bath, Haircut, Dressmaking, Meeting friends, Start a construction, Setting up a bed, Adopting animals, Funeral.
Avoid: Wedding, Moving to a new house.

Weekly review/ gratitude:

July 2022

Week 29

July

S	M	T	W	T	F	S
26	27	28	29	30	1	2
3	4	5	6	7	8	9
10	11	12	13	14	15	16
17	18	19	20	21	22	23
24	25	26	27	28	29	30
31	1	2	3	4	5	6

---

11 (lunar date: 06/13)

Monday
Yi Chou (乙丑) - Metal

Happiness star: **Northwest**, Wealth star: **Southeast**
Conflicting sign: **Goat,** Conflicting direction: **East**

Lucky: Ceremony, Demolition.
Avoid: Any major festive event.

---

12 (06/14)

Tuesday
Bing Yin (丙寅) - Fire

Happiness star: **Southwest**, Wealth star: **West**
Conflicting sign: **Monkey,** Conflicting direction: **North**

Lucky: Wedding, Dressmaking, Starting a construction, Setting up a bed, Moving to a new house, Funeral, Planting, Adopting animals.
Avoid: Sharp knives, Travel, Activating Feng Shui cures.

---

13 (06/15)

Wednesday
Ding Mao (丁卯) - Fire

Happiness star: **South,** Wealth star: **West**
Conflicting sign: **Rooster,** Conflicting direction: **West**

Lucky: Ceremony, Travel, Starting a construction, Moving to a new house, Starting a business, Funeral, Planting, Adopting animals.
Avoid: Sharp knives, Activating Feng Shui cures, Wedding.

---

14 (06/16)

Thursday
Wu Chen (戊辰) - Wood

Happiness star: **Southeast**, Wealth star: **North**
Conflicting sign: **Dog,** Conflicting direction: **South**

Lucky: Ceremony, Setting up a stove.
Avoid: Wedding, Moving to a new house, Setting up a bed, Starting a business.

Weekly goals/ to do:

_____

_____

_____

_____

15 (06/17)   **Friday**

Happiness star: **Northeast**, Wealth star: **North**   Ji Si (己巳) - Wood

Conflicting sign: **Pig,** Conflicting direction: **East**

Lucky: Ceremony, Activating Feng Shui cures, Dressmaking, Meeting friends, Starting a construction, Setting up a stove/bed/door, Starting a business.

Avoid: Wedding, Adopting animals, Funeral.

16 (06/18)   Saturday

Happiness star: **Northwest**, Wealth star: **East**   Geng Wu (庚午) - Earth

Conflicting sign: **Rat,** Conflicting direction: **North**

Lucky: Ceremony, Pest control, Funeral.

Avoid: Any major festive event.

17 (06/19)   Sunday

Happiness star: **Southwest**, Wealth star: **East**   Xin Wei (辛未) - Earth

Conflicting sign: **Ox,** Conflicting direction: **West**

Lucky: Ceremony, Travel, Wedding, Dressmaking, Moving to a new house, Setting up a bed/door, Adopting animals, Signing a contract, Meeting friends.

Avoid: Starting a construction, Starting a business, Funeral.

Weekly review/ gratitude:

_____

_____

_____

_____

July 2022

Week 30

July

S	M	T	W	T	F	S
26	27	28	29	30	1	2
3	4	5	6	7	8	9
10	11	12	13	14	15	16
17	18	19	20	21	22	23
24	25	26	27	28	29	30
31	1	2	3	4	5	6

---

18 (lunar date: 06/20)   **Monday**
Happiness star: **South**, Wealth star: **South**   Ren Shen (壬申) - Metal
Conflicting sign: **Tiger**, Conflicting direction: **South**

Lucky: Ceremony, Activating Feng Shui cures, Bath, Wedding, House cleaning, Funeral, Visiting a doctor.
Avoid: Moving to a new house, Starting a business.

---

19 (06/21)   **Tuesday**
Happiness star: **Southeast**, Wealth star: **South**   Kui You (癸酉) - Metal
Conflicting sign: **Rabbit**, Conflicting direction: **East**

Lucky: Ceremony, Travel, Bath, Wedding, Dressmaking, Setting up a bed, Starting a business, Activating Feng Shui cures, Adopting animals, Funeral.
Avoid: Starting a construction, Moving to a new house.

---

20 (06/22)   **Wednesday**
Happiness star: **Northeast**, Wealth star: **Southeast**   Jia Xu (甲戌) - Fire
Conflicting sign: **Dragon**, Conflicting direction: **North**

Lucky: Ceremony, Wedding, Dressmaking, Bath, Fishing.
Avoid: Starting a construction, Activating Feng Shui cures, Moving to a new house, Funeral.

---

21 (06/23)   **Thursday**
Happiness star: **Northwest**, Wealth star: **Southwest**   Yi Hai (乙亥) - Fire
Conflicting sign: **Snake**, Conflicting direction: **West**

Lucky: Bath, Dressmaking, Moving to a new house, Setting up a bed/stove, Starting a business.
Avoid: Wedding, Activating Feng Shui cures, Funeral.

Weekly goals/ to do:

_____
_____
_____
_____

22 (06/24)   **Friday**
Happiness star: **Southwest**, Wealth star: **West**   Bing Zi (丙子) - Water
Conflicting sign: **Horse**, Conflicting direction: **South**

Lucky: Ceremony, Removing Feng Shui cures, Bath, Haircut, Funeral.
Avoid: Wedding, Moving to a new house, Travel.

23 (06/25) * *Greater Heat (Da Shu 大暑)*   Saturday
Happiness star: **South**, Wealth star: **West**   Ding Chou (丁丑) - Water
Conflicting sign: **Goat,** Conflicting direction: **East**

Lucky: Ceremony, Demolition.
Avoid: Any major festive event.

24 (06/26)   Sunday
Happiness star: **Southeast**, Wealth star: **North**   Wu Yin (戊寅) - Earth
Conflicting sign: **Monkey,** Conflicting direction: **North**

Lucky: Travel, Wedding, Dressmaking, Setting up a bed/stove, Funeral, Moving to a new house,
Starting a business, Adopting animals, Planting.
Avoid: Sharp knives, Activating Feng Shui cures.

Weekly review/ gratitude:

_____
_____
_____
_____
_____

July 2022

Week 31

July

S	M	T	W	T	F	S
26	27	28	29	30	1	2
3	4	5	6	7	8	9
10	11	12	13	14	15	16
17	18	19	20	21	22	23
24	25	26	27	28	29	30
31	1	2	3	4	5	6

---

25 (lunar date: 06/27)

Monday

Ji Mao (己卯) - Earth

Happiness star: **Northeast,** Wealth star: **North**

Conflicting sign: **Rooster,** Conflicting direction: **West**

Lucky: Ceremony, Travel, Wedding, Setting up a bed/stove, Starting a business, Trading, Planting, Adopting animals, Visiting a doctor.

Avoid: Sharp knives, Visiting sick patients, Activating Feng Shui cures.

---

26 (06/28)

Tuesday

Geng Chen (庚辰) - Metal

Happiness star: **Northwest,** Wealth star: **East**

Conflicting sign: **Dog,** Conflicting direction: **South**

Lucky: Ceremony, Setting up a stove, Planting, Hunting, Adopting animals.

Avoid: Wedding, Setting up a bed, Moving to a new house, Funeral.

---

27 (06/29)

Wednesday

Xin Si (辛巳) - Metal

Happiness star: **Southwest,** Wealth star: **East**

Conflicting sign: **Pig,** Conflicting direction: **East**

Lucky: Ceremony, Activating Feng Shui cures, Wedding, Starting a business, Visiting a doctor.

Avoid: Moving to a new house, Funeral.

---

28 (06/30)

Thursday

Ren Wu (壬午) - Wood

Happiness star: **South,** Wealth star: **South**

Conflicting sign: **Rat,** Conflicting direction: **North**

Lucky: Ceremony, Funeral.

Avoid: Any major festive event, Visiting sick patients.

29 (07/01)

Happiness star: **Southeast,** Wealth star: **South**

Conflicting sign: **Ox,** Conflicting direction: **West**

Friday

Kui Wei (癸未) - Wood

Lucky: Ceremony, Travel, Dressmaking, Meeting friends, Trading, Fixing animal houses.

Avoid: Wedding, Moving to a new house, Activating Feng Shui cures, Funeral.

30 (07/02)

Happiness star: **Northeast,** Wealth star: **Southeast**

Conflicting sign: **Tiger,** Conflicting direction: **South**

Saturday

Jia Shen (甲申) - Water

Lucky: Ceremony, Activating Feng Shui cures, Starting a business, Planting, Adopting animals, Funeral.

Avoid: Wedding, Moving to a new house.

31 (07/03)

Happiness star: **Northwest,** Wealth star: **Southeast**

Conflicting sign: **Rabbit,** Conflicting direction: **East**

Sunday

Yi You (乙酉) - Water

Lucky: Ceremony, Bath, Haircut, Dressmaking, Wedding, Starting a business, Travel, Adopting animals, Funeral.

Avoid: Moving to a new house, Activating Feng Shui cures.

Weekly review/ gratitude:

August 2022

Week 32

August

S	M	T	W	T	F	S
31	1	2	3	4	5	6
7	8	9	10	11	12	13
14	15	16	17	18	19	20
21	22	23	24	25	26	27
28	29	30	31	1	2	3

Aug 1 (lunar date: 07/04)

Monday
Bing Xu (丙戌) - Earth

Happiness star: **Southwest**, Wealth star: **West**

Conflicting sign: **Dragon**, Conflicting direction: **North**

Lucky: Ceremony, Hunting, Fishing.
Avoid: Moving to a new house, Wedding, Starting a construction, Funeral.

---

2 (07/05)

Tuesday
Ding Hai (丁亥) - Earth

Happiness star: **South**, Wealth star: **West**

Conflicting sign: **Snake**, Conflicting direction: **West**

Lucky: Ceremony, Activating Feng Shui cures, Bath, Dressmaking, Meeting friends, Setting up a bed/door, Moving to a new house, Adopting animals.
Avoid: Wedding, Funeral, Travel.

---

3 (07/06)

Wednesday
Wu Zi (戊子) - Fire

Happiness star: **Southeast**, Wealth star: **North**

Conflicting sign: **Horse**, Conflicting direction: **South**

Lucky: Ceremony, Removing Feng Shui cures, Bath, Haircut, Training animals, Fishing, Funeral.
Avoid: Wedding, Starting a business.

---

4 (07/07) *Chinese Valentine's Day*

Thursday
Ji Chou (己丑) - Fire

Happiness star: **Northeast**, Wealth star: **North**

Conflicting sign: **Goat**, Conflicting direction: **East**

Lucky: Ceremony, Demolition.
Avoid: Any major festive event.

---

5 (07/08)   **Friday**
                                                   Geng Yin (庚寅) - Wood

Happiness star: **Northwest**, Wealth star: **East**
Conflicting sign: **Monkey**, Conflicting direction: **North**

Lucky: Activating Feng Shui cures, Travel, Signing a contract, Wedding, Meeting friends,
Planting, Funeral.
Avoid: Sharp knives, Moving to a new house, Starting a business.

---

6 (07/09)   Saturday
                                                   Xin Mao (辛卯) - Wood

Happiness star: **Southwest**, Wealth star: **East**
Conflicting sign: **Rooster**, Conflicting direction: **West**

Lucky: Ceremony, Funeral, Planting, Adopting animals, Visiting a doctor.
Avoid: Sharp knives, Wedding, Moving to a new house.

---

7 (07/10) * *Start of Autumn (Li Qiu 立秋)*   Sunday
                                                   Ren Chen (壬辰) - Water

Happiness star: **South**, Wealth star: **South**
Conflicting sign: **Dog**, Conflicting direction: **South**

Lucky: Ceremony, Setting up a stove, Planting, Fishing.
Avoid: Wedding, Setting up a bed, Starting a business.

Weekly review/ gratitude:

August 2022

Week 33

August

S	M	T	W	T	F	S
31	1	2	3	4	5	6
7	8	9	10	11	12	13
14	15	16	17	18	19	20
21	22	23	24	25	26	27
28	29	30	31	1	2	3

---

8 (lunar date: 07/11)   **Monday**

Happiness star: **Southeast**, Wealth star: **South**   Kui Si (癸巳) - Water

Conflicting sign: **Pig,** Conflicting direction: **East**

Lucky: Ceremony, Wedding, Dressmaking, Starting a construction, Moving to a new house, Setting up a bed/stove, Starting a business, Planting.

Avoid: Sharp knives, Funeral.

---

9 (07/12)   **Tuesday**

Happiness star: **Northeast**, Wealth star: **Southeast**   Jia Wu (甲午) - Metal

Conflicting sign: **Rat,** Conflicting direction: **North**

Lucky: Ceremony, Activating Feng Shui cures, Travel, Haircut, Signing a contract, Dressmaking, Wedding, Meeting friends, Starting a construction, Setting up a bed, Starting a business.

Avoid: Sharp knives, Moving to a new house, Funeral.

---

10 (07/13)   **Wednesday**

Happiness star: **Northwest**, Wealth star: **Southeast**   Yi Wei (乙未) - Metal

Conflicting sign: **Ox,** Conflicting direction: **West**

Lucky: Ceremony, Dressmaking, Wedding, Setting up a door/stove/bed, Moving to a new house.

Avoid: Activating Feng Shui cures, Starting a construction, Funeral.

---

11 (07/14)   **Thursday**

Happiness star: **Southwest**, Wealth star: **West**   Bing Shen (丙申) - Fire

Conflicting sign: **Tiger,** Conflicting direction: **South**

Lucky: Ceremony, Bath, Dressmaking, Wedding, House cleaning, Adopting animals, Funeral.

Avoid: Setting up a bed/stove.

Weekly goals/ to do:

_____

_____

_____

_____

12 (07/15)   **Friday**
                                                  Ding You (丁酉) - Fire

Happiness star: **South**, Wealth star: **West**
Conflicting sign: **Rabbit**, Conflicting direction: **East**

Lucky: Ceremony, Starting a construction, Signing a contract, Dressmaking, Setting up a door/
bed, House cleaning, Adopting animals, Funeral.
Avoid: Wedding, Moving to anew house, Activating Feng Shui cures.

13 (07/16)   Saturday
                                                  Wu Xu (戊戌) - Wood

Happiness star: **Southeast**, Wealth star: **North**
Conflicting sign: **Dragon**, Conflicting direction: **North**

Lucky: Activating Feng Shui cures, Travel, Dressmaking, Meeting friends, Setting up a bed,
Moving to a new house, Starting a business, Trading, Adopting animals, Visiting a doctor.
Avoid: Wedding, Funeral.

14 (07/17)   Sunday
                                                  Ji Hai (己亥) - Wood

Happiness star: **Northeast**, Wealth star: **North**
Conflicting sign: **Snake**, Conflicting direction: **West**

Lucky: Ceremony, Bath, Fixing a street/walkway.
Avoid: Wedding.

Weekly review/ gratitude:

_____

_____

_____

_____

August 2022

Week 34

August

S	M	T	W	T	F	S
31	1	2	3	4	5	6
7	8	9	10	11	12	13
14	15	16	17	18	19	20
21	22	23	24	25	26	27
28	29	30	31	1	2	3

---

15 (lunar date: 07/18) **Monday**
Geng Zi (庚子) - Earth

Happiness star: **Northwest**, Wealth star: **East**

Conflicting sign: **Horse**, Conflicting direction: **South**

Lucky: Ceremony, Activating Feng Shui cures, Adopting animals, Dressmaking, Starting a construction, Setting up a bed/door.

Avoid: Wedding, Moving to a new house, Signing a contract, Setting up a stove.

---

16 (07/19) **Tuesday**
Xin Chou (辛丑) - Earth

Happiness star: **Southwest**, Wealth star: **East**

Conflicting sign: **Goat,** Conflicting direction: **East**

Lucky: Funeral, Fishing, Pest control.

Avoid: Any major festive event.

---

17 (07/20) **Wednesday**
Ren Yin (壬寅) - Metal

Happiness star: **South**, Wealth star: **South**

Conflicting sign: **Monkey,** Conflicting direction: **North**

Lucky: Bath, Demolition, Visiting a doctor.

Avoid: **Any major festive event,** Visitng sick patients.

---

18 (07/21) **Thursday**
Kui Mao (癸卯) - Metal

Happiness star: **Southeast**, Wealth star: **South**

Conflicting sign: **Rooster** Conflicting direction: **west**

Lucky: Ceremony, Activating Feng Shui cures, Travel, Dressmaking, Wedding, Moving to a new house, Starting a business, Adopting animals, Funeral.

Avoid: Starting a construction, Setting up a bed or door.

Weekly goals/ to do:

_____
_____
_____
_____

19 (07/22)   **Friday**

Happiness star: **Northeast**, Wealth star: **Southeast**   Jia Chen (甲辰) - Fire

Conflicting sign: **Dog,** Conflicting direction: **South**

Lucky: Ceremony, Activating Feng Shui cures, Wedding, Starting a construction, Setting up a stove, Moving to a new house, Hunting, Fishing Funeral.

Avoid: Starting a business, Setting up a door.

20 (07/23)   Saturday

Happiness star: **Northwest**, Wealth star: **Southeast**   Yi Si (乙巳) - Fire

Conflicting sign: **Pig,** Conflicting direction: **East**

Lucky: Ceremony, Meeting friends, Setting up a bed/stove, Dressmaking, Starting a business, Trading, Adopting animals.

Avoid: Sharp knives, Wedding, Funeral, Activating Feng Shui cures, Moving to a new house.

21 (07/24)   Sunday

Happiness star: **Southwest**, Wealth star: **West**   Rbing Wu (丙午) - Water

Conflicting sign: **Rat,** Conflicting direction: **North**

Lucky: Ceremony, Travel, Activating Feng Shui cures, Dressmaking, Wedding, Starting a construction, Setting up a bed, Visiting a doctor, Signing a contract.

Avoid: Sharp knives, Moving to a new house, Funeral.

Weekly review/ gratitude:

_____
_____
_____
_____
_____

August 2022

Week 35

August

S	M	T	W	T	F	S
31	1	2	3	4	5	6
7	8	9	10	11	12	13
14	15	16	17	18	19	20
21	22	23	24	25	26	27
28	29	30	31	1	2	3

---

22 (lunar date: 07/25)   **Monday**
Ding Wei (丁未) - Water

Happiness star: **South,** Wealth star: **West**

Conflicting sign: **Ox,** Conflicting direction: **West**

Lucky: Ceremony, Travel, Adopting animals, Starting a construction, Setting up a bed, Visiting a doctor, Funeral.
Avoid: Wedding, Activating Feng Shui cures, Moving to a new house.

---

23 (07/26) ** Hidden Summer (Chu Shu 處暑)*   **Tuesday**
Wu Shen (戊申) - Earth

Happiness star: **Southeast,** Wealth star: **North**

Conflicting sign: **Tiger,** Conflicting direction: **South**

Lucky: Ceremony, Travel, Bath, Activating Feng Shui cures, Dressmaking, Meeting friends, Adopting animals, Visiting a doctor, Funeral.
Avoid: Wedding, Starting a construction.

---

24 (07/27)   **Wednesday**
Ji You (己酉) - Earth

Happiness star: **Northeast,** Wealth star: **North**

Conflicting sign: **Rabbit,** Conflicting direction: **East**

Lucky: Ceremony, Removing Feng Shui cures, Bath, Haircut, House cleaning, Hunting, Planting, Adopting animals, Starting a construction, Funeral.
Avoid: Wedding, Moving to a new house, Activating Feng Shui cures, Starting a business.

---

25 (07/28)   **Thursday**
Geng Xu (庚戌) - Metal

Happiness star: **Northwest,** Wealth star: **East**

Conflicting sign: **Dragon,** Conflicting direction: **North**

Lucky: Activating Feng Shui cures, Wedding, Meeting friends, Pest control, Planting, Hunting, Adopting animals.
Avoid: Wedding, Starting a construction, Moving to a new house, Funeral.

26 (07/29)

Friday

Xin Hai (辛亥) - Metal

Happiness star: **Southwest**, Wealth star: **East**
Conflicting sign: **Snake**, Conflicting direction: **West**

Lucky: Ceremony, Setting up a stove.
Avoid: Moving to a new house, Wedding, Funeral.

27 (08/01)

Saturday

Ren Zi (壬子) - Wood

Happiness star: **South**, Wealth star: **South**
Conflicting sign: **Horse**, Conflicting direction: **South**

Lucky: Ceremony, Activating Feng Shui cures, Travel, Adopting animals, Starting a construction, Moving to a new house, Setting up a bed, Funeral.
Avoid: Starting a business, Wedding.

28 (08/02)

Sunday

Kui Chou (癸丑) - Wood

Happiness star: **Southeast**, Wealth star: **South**
Conflicting sign: **Goat**, Conflicting direction: **East**

Lucky: Ceremony, Funeral.
Avoid: Any major festive event.

Weekly review/ gratitude:

August - September 2022

Week 36

September

S	M	T	W	T	F	S
28	29	30	31	1	2	3
4	5	6	7	8	9	10
11	12	13	14	15	16	17
18	19	20	21	22	23	24
25	26	27	28	29	30	1

---

29 (lunar date: 08/03)

Monday

Jia Yin (甲寅) - Water

Happiness star: **Northeast**, Wealth star: **Southeast**

Conflicting sign: **Monkey**, Conflicting direction: **North**

Lucky: Demolition.

Avoid: Any major festive event, visiting sick patients.

---

30 (08/04)

Tuesday

Yi Mao (乙卯) - Water

Happiness star: **Northwest**, Wealth star: **Southeast**

Conflicting sign: **Rooster**, Conflicting direction: **West**

Lucky: Ceremony, Hunting, Fishing, Funeral.

Avoid: Wedding, Moving to a new house, Starting a construction, Setting up a bed/stove, Visiting sick patients.

---

31 (08/05)

Wednesday

Bing Chen (丙辰) - Earth

Happiness star: **Southwest**, Wealth star: **West**

Conflicting sign: **Dog**, Conflicting direction: **South**

Lucky: Ceremony, Wedding, Setting up a bed, Moving to a new house, Funeral, Visiting a doctor.

Avoid: Travel, Setting up a stove.

Sep 1 (08/06)

Thursday

Ding Si (丁巳) - Earth

Happiness star: **South**, Wealth star: **West**

Conflicting sign: **Pig**, Conflicting direction: **East**

Lucky: Ceremony, Dressmaking, Wedding, Setting up a bed, Moving to a new house, Meeting friends, Trading, Adopting animals.

Avoid: Sharp knives, Activating Feng Shui cures, Funeral.

---

2 (08/07)   **Friday**

Happiness star: **Southeast**, Wealth star: **North**   Wu Wu (戊午) - Fire
Conflicting sign: **Rat,** Conflicting direction: **North**

Lucky: Ceremony, Travel, Signing a contract, Meeting friends, Setting up a bed, Starting a business, Planting, Dressmaking, Visiting a doctor.
Avoid: Sharp knives, Moving to a new house, Activating Feng Shui cures, Starting a construction, Funeral.

---

3 (08/08)   Saturday

Happiness star: **Northeast**, Wealth star: **North**   Ji Wei (己未) - Fire
Conflicting sign: **Ox,** Conflicting direction: **West**

Lucky: Ceremony, Meeting friends, Starting a construction, Pest control, Wedding.
Avoid: Moving to a new house, Funeral, Activating Feng Shui cures, Travel.

---

4 (08/09)   Sunday

Happiness star: **Northwest**, Wealth star: **East**   Geng Shen (庚申) - Wood
Conflicting sign: **Tiger,** Conflicting direction: **South**

Lucky: None.
Avoid: Any major festive event.

Weekly review/ gratitude:

September 2022

Week 37

September

S	M	T	W	T	F	S
28	29	30	31	1	2	3
4	5	6	7	8	9	10
11	12	13	14	15	16	17
18	19	20	21	22	23	24
25	26	27	28	29	30	1

---

5 (lunar date: 08/10)   **Monday**
                                                       Xin You (辛酉) - Wood

Happiness star: **Southwest**, Wealth star: **East**

Conflicting sign: **Rabbit,** Conflicting direction: **East**

Lucky: Ceremony, Bath, Haircut, Starting a construction, Setting up a bed, House cleaning, Funeral, Dressmaking.

Avoid: Wedding, Moving to a new house, Starting a business.

---

6 (08/11)   **Tuesday**
                                                       Ren Wu (壬戌) - Water

Happiness star: **South**, Wealth star: **South**

Conflicting sign: **Dragon,** Conflicting direction: **North**

Lucky: Travel, Activating Feng Shui cures, Dressmaking, Wedding, Setting up a bed, Moving to a new house, Starting a business, Trading, Planting, Adopting animals, Visiting a doctor.

Avoid: Starting a construction, Funeral.

---

7 (08/12) * *White Dew (Bai Lu 白露)*   **Wednesday**
                                                       Kui Hai (癸亥) - Water

Happiness star: **Southeast**, Wealth star: **South**

Conflicting sign: **Snake,** Conflicting direction: **West**

Lucky: Ceremony, Bath, Setting up a stove.

Avoid: Wedding, Moving to a new house, Funeral.

---

8 (08/13)   **Thursday**
                                                       Jia Zi (甲子) - Metal

Happiness star: **Northeast**, Wealth star: **Southeast**

Conflicting sign: **Horse,** Conflicting direction: **South**

Lucky: Ceremony, Bath, Fixing street/walkway.

Avoid: Wedding, Moving to a new house, Funeral, Dressmaking.

Weekly goals/ to do:

_____

_____

_____

_____

9 (08/14)   **Friday**
                                                         Yi Chou (乙丑) - Metal
Happiness star: **Northwest**, Wealth star: **Southeast**
Conflicting sign: **Goat** Conflicting direction: **East**

Lucky: Adopting animals, Wedding, Starting a construction, Setting up a stove/bed, Moving to a new house, Funeral.
Avoid: Activating Feng Shui cures.

10 (08/15) * *Moon Festival*   Saturday
                                                         Bing Yin (丙寅) - Fire
Happiness star: **Southwest**, Wealth star: **West**
Conflicting sign: **Monkey,** Conflicting direction: **North**

Lucky: Ceremony, Meeting friends, Setting up a door, Funeral.
Avoid: Wedding, Activating Feng Shui cures, Moving to a new house.

11 (08/16)   Sunday
                                                         Ding Mao (丁卯) - Fire
Happiness star: **South**, Wealth star: **West**
Conflicting sign: **Rooster,** Conflicting direction: **West**

Lucky: Ceremony, Demolition, Bath, Visiting a doctor.
Avoid: Any major festive event.

Weekly review/ gratitude:

_____

_____

_____

_____

September 2022

Week 38

September

S	M	T	W	T	F	S
28	29	30	31	1	2	3
4	5	6	7	8	9	10
11	12	13	14	15	16	17
18	19	20	21	22	23	24
25	26	27	28	29	30	1

---

12 (lunar date: 08/17)   **Monday**
                                          Wu Chen (戊辰) - Wood

Happiness star: **Southeast** Wealth star: **North**

Conflicting sign: **Dog,** Conflicting direction: **South**

Lucky: Ceremony, Travel, Activating Feng Shui cures, Haircut, Dressmaking, Setting up a bed/stove, Moving to a new house, Starting a business, Trading.
Avoid: Wedding, Funeral.

---

13 (08/18)   **Tuesday**
                                             Ji Si (己巳) - Wood

Happiness star: **Northeast,** Wealth star: **North**

Conflicting sign: **Pig,** Conflicting direction: **East**

Lucky: Ceremony, Wedding, Starting a construction, Setting up a bed/stove, Moving to a new house, Planting.
Avoid: Sharp knives, Funeral.

---

14 (08/19)   **Wednesday**
                                          Geng Wu (庚午) - Earth

Happiness star: **Northwest,** Wealth star: **East**

Conflicting sign: **Rat,** Conflicting direction: **North**

Lucky: Ceremony, Haircut, Wedding.
Avoid: Sharp knives, Starting a business, Moving to a new house, Funeral.

---

15 (08/20)   **Thursday**
                                           Xin Wei (辛未) - Earth

Happiness star: **Southwest,** Wealth star: **East**

Conflicting sign: **Ox,** Conflicting direction: **West**

Lucky: Ceremony.
Avoid: Any major festive event.

16 (08/21)

Friday
Ren Shen (壬申) - Metal

Happiness star: **South**, Wealth star: **South**
Conflicting sign: **Tiger**, Conflicting direction: **South**

Lucky: Ceremony, Bath, Haircut, Wedding, Dressmaking, Starting a construction, Planting, Adopting animals, Moving to a new house, Funeral.
Avoid: Setting up a door.

17 (08/22)

Saturday
Kui You (癸酉) - Metal

Happiness star: **Southeast**, Wealth star: **South**
Conflicting sign: **Rabbit**, Conflicting direction: **East**

Lucky: Ceremony, Travel, Bath, House cleaning.
Avoid: Start a construction, Starting a business, Wedding, Activating Feng Shui cures, Moving to a new house.

18 (08/23)

Sunday
Jia Xu (甲戌) - Fire

Happiness star: **Northeast**, Wealth star: **Southeast**
Conflicting sign: **Dragon**, Conflicting direction: **North**

Lucky: Ceremony, Travel, Bath, Haircut, Dressmaking, Starting a construction, Setting up a bed, House cleaning, Moving to a new house, Starting a business.
Avoid: Wedding, Activating Feng Shui cures, Funeral.

Weekly review/ gratitude:

September 2022

Week 39

September

S	M	T	W	T	F	S
28	29	30	31	1	2	3
4	5	6	7	8	9	10
11	12	13	14	15	16	17
18	19	20	21	22	23	24
25	26	27	28	29	30	1

---

19 (lunar date: 08/24)   **Monday**
                                                      Yi Hai (乙亥) - Fire

Happiness star: **Northwest**, Wealth star: **Southeast**
Conflicting sign: **Snake**, Conflicting direction: **West**

Lucky: Ceremony, Activating Feng Shui cures, Travel, Setting up a bed/stove, Moving to a new house, Adopting animals, Starting a business, Fishing, Adopting animals, Visiting a doctor.
Avoid: Wedding.

---

20 (08/25)   **Tuesday**
                                                     Bing Zi (丙子) - Water

Happiness star: **Southwest**, Wealth star: **West**
Conflicting sign: **Horse**, Conflicting direction: **South**

Lucky: Ceremony, Bath.
Avoid: Wedding, Moving to a new house, Travel, Funeral.

---

21 (08/26)   **Wednesday**
                                                   Ding Chou (丁丑) - Water

Happiness star: **South**, Wealth star: **West**
Conflicting sign: **Goat**, Conflicting direction: **East**

Lucky: Ceremony, Travel, Adopting animals, Wedding, Starting a construction, Setting up a bed/stove, Moving to a new house, Starting a business, Funeral.
Avoid: Activating Feng Shui cures.

---

22 (08/27)   **Thursday**
                                                     Wu Yin (戊寅) - Earth

Happiness star: **Southeast**, Wealth star: **North**
Conflicting sign: **Monkey**, Conflicting direction: **North**

Lucky: Activating Feng Shui cures, Dressmaking, Funeral.
Avoid: Travel, Wedding, Any major festive event.

---

23 (08/28) ** Autumn Equinox (Qiu Fen 秋分)*

Happiness star: **Northeast**, Wealth star: **North**

Conflicting sign: **Rooster,** Conflicting direction: **West**

Friday

Ji Mao (己卯) - Earth

Lucky: Demolition, Visiting a doctor.

Avoid: Any major festive event, visiting sick patients.

---

24 (08/29)

Happiness star: **Northwest**, Wealth star: **East**

Conflicting sign: **Dog,** Conflicting direction: **South**

Saturday

Geng Chen (庚辰) - Metal

Lucky: Ceremony, Activating Feng Shui cures, Start a construction, Setting up a bed/stove, Starting a business, Funeral, Dressmaking, Planting.

Avoid: Wedding, Moving to a new house.

---

25 (08/30)

Happiness star: **Southwest**, Wealth star: **East**

Conflicting sign: **Pig,** Conflicting direction: **East**

Sunday

Xin Si (辛巳) - Metal

Lucky: Ceremony, Wedding, Starting a construction, Moving to a new house, Trading, Planting, Adopting animals.

Avoid: Activating Feng Shui cures, Funeral.

Weekly review/ gratitude:

September - October 2022

Week 40

September

S	M	T	W	T	F	S
28	29	30	31	1	2	3
4	5	6	7	8	9	10
11	12	13	14	15	16	17
18	19	20	21	22	23	24
25	26	27	28	29	30	1

---

26 (lunar date: 09/01)   **Monday**
Happiness star: **South**, Wealth star: **South**   Ren Wu (壬午) - Wood
Conflicting sign: **Rat,** Conflicting direction: **North**

Lucky: Ceremony, Haircut, Meeting friends, Training animals.
Avoid: Wedding, Activating Feng Shui cures, Moving to a new house, Starting a business, Funeral, Dressmaking, Setting up a stove, Sharp knives, Visiting sick patients.

---

27 (09/02)   **Tuesday**
Happiness star: **Southeast**, Wealth star: **South**   Kui Wei (癸未) - Wood
Conflicting sign: **Ox**, Conflicting direction: **West**

Lucky: Ceremony, Meeting friends.
Avoid: Any major festive event.

---

28 (09/03)   **Wednesday**
Happiness star: **Northeast**, Wealth star: **Southeast**   Jia Shen (甲申) - Water
Conflicting sign: **Tiger**, Conflicting direction: **South**

Lucky: Ceremony, Travel, Bath, Wedding, Planting, Funeral.
Avoid: Activating Feng Shui cures, Moving to a new house.

---

29 (09/04)   **Thursday**
Happiness star: **Northwest**, Wealth star: **Southeast**   Yi You (乙酉) - Water
Conflicting sign: **Rabbit**, Conflicting direction: **East**

Lucky: Travel, Ceremony, Bath, House cleaning, Funeral.
Avoid: Starting a business, Starting a construction, Moving to a new house.

Weekly goals/ to do:

_____

_____

_____

_____

---

30 (09/05)   **Friday**
                                          Bing Xu (丙戌) - Earth
Happiness star: **Southwest**, Wealth star: **West**
Conflicting sign: **Dragon,** Conflicting direction: **North**

Lucky: Ceremony, Activating Feng Shui cures, Bath, Haircut, Dressmaking, Wedding, Starting a construction, Setting up a bed, House cleaning, Planting.
Avoid: Funeral.

Oct 1 (09/06)   Saturday
                                          Ding Hai (丁亥) - Earth
Happiness star: **South**, Wealth star: **West**
Conflicting sign: **Snake,** Conflicting direction: **West**

Lucky: Ceremony, Travel, Activating Feng Shui cures, Dressmaking, Setting up a bed, Moving to a new house, Starting a business, Bath, Meeting friends, Trading.
Avoid: Starting a construction, Wedding, Funeral.

---

2 (09/07)   Sunday
                                          Wu Zi (戊子) - Fire
Happiness star: **Southeast**, Wealth star: **North**
Conflicting sign: **Horse,** Conflicting direction: **South**

Lucky: Ceremony, Bath, Fixing walls/walkway.
Avoid: Wedding, Moving to a new house, Activating Feng Shui cures, Travel.

Weekly review/ gratitude:

_____

_____

_____

_____

October 2022

Week 41

October

S	M	T	W	T	F	S
25	26	27	28	29	30	1
2	3	4	5	6	7	8
9	10	11	12	13	14	15
16	17	18	19	20	21	22
23	24	25	26	27	28	29
30	31	1	2	3	4	5

---

3 (lunar date: 09/08)   **Monday**

Happiness star: **Northeast** Wealth star: **North**   Ji Chou (己丑) - Fire

Conflicting sign: **Goat**, Conflicting direction: **East**

Lucky: Ceremony, Travel, Activating Feng Shui cures, Wedding, Starting a construction, Setting up a stove, Moving to a new house, Starting a business, Funeral.
Avoid: Setting up a door/bed.

---

4 (09/09)   **Tuesday**

Happiness star: **Northwest**, Wealth star: **East**   Geng Yin (庚寅) - Wood

Conflicting sign: **Monkey**, Conflicting direction: **North**

Lucky: Signing a contract, Dressmaking, Meeting friends, Starting a construction, Funeral.
Avoid: Wedding, Moving to a new house, Activating Feng Shui cures.

---

5 (09/10)   **Wednesday**

Happiness star: **Southwest**, Wealth star: **East**   Xin Mao (辛卯) - Wood

Conflicting sign: **Rooster**, Conflicting direction: **west**

Lucky: Ceremony, Demolition, Visiting a doctor.
Avoid: Any major festive event.

---

6 (09/11)   **Thursday**

Happiness star: **South**, Wealth star: **South**   Ren Chen (壬辰) - Water

Conflicting sign: **Dog**, Conflicting direction: **South**

Lucky: Ceremony, Travel, Wedding, Dressmaking, Starting a business, Starting a construction, Setting up a door/stove, Moving to a new house, Trading, Funeral.
Avoid: Adopting animals.

7 (09/12)   **Friday**

Happiness star: **Southeast**, Wealth star: **South**   Kui Si (癸巳) - Water

Conflicting sign: **Pig,** Conflicting direction: **East**

Lucky: Ceremony, Activating Feng Shui cures, Wedding, Starting a construction, Setting up a stove, Moving to a new house, Starting a business, Visiting a doctor.

Avoid: Sharp knives, Funeral.

---

8 (09/13) * *Cold Dew (Han Lu 寒露)*   Saturday

Happiness star: **Northeast**, Wealth star: **Southeast**   Jia Wu (甲午) - Metal

Conflicting sign: **Rat,** Conflicting direction: **North**

Lucky: Ceremony, Haircut, Wedding, Meeting friends, Setting up a stove, Trading, Funeral.

Avoid: Sharp knives.

---

9 (09/14)   Sunday

Happiness star: **Northwest**, Wealth star: **Southeast**   Yi Wei (乙未) - Metal

Conflicting sign: **Ox,** Conflicting direction: **West**

Lucky: Ceremony, Wedding, Setting up a stove, Hunting.

Avoid: Starting a construction, Starting a business, Funeral.

Weekly review/ gratitude:

October 2022

Week 42

October

S	M	T	W	T	F	S
25	26	27	28	29	30	1
2	3	4	5	6	7	8
9	10	11	12	13	14	15
16	17	18	19	20	21	22
23	24	25	26	27	28	29
30	31	1	2	3	4	5

---

10 (lunar date: 09/15)   **Monday**

Happiness star: **Southwest**, Wealth star: **West**   Bing Shen (丙申) - Fire

Conflicting sign: **Tiger,** Conflicting direction: **South**

Lucky: Ceremony, Travel, Adopting animals, Starting a construction, Moving to a new house, Setting up a door, Stating a business.

Avoid: Wedding, Setting up a stove.

---

11 (09/16)   **Tuesday**

Happiness star: **South**, Wealth star: **West**   Ding You (丁酉) - Fire

Conflicting sign: **Rabbit,** Conflicting direction: **East**

Lucky: Ceremony, Bath, Wedding, Setting up a bed, Funeral, Fixing animal houses.

Avoid: Starting a business, Setting up a door, Activating Feng Shui cures.

---

12 (09/17)   **Wednesday**

Happiness star: **Southeast**, Wealth star: **North**   Wu Xu (戊戌) - Wood

Conflicting sign: **Dragon,** Conflicting direction: **North**

Lucky: Fixing animal houses.

Avoid: Start a construction, Wedding, Moving to a new house, Funeral.

---

13 (09/18)   **Thursday**

Happiness star: **Northeast**, Wealth star: **North**   Yi Hai (己亥) - Wood

Conflicting sign: **Snake,** Conflicting direction: **West**

Lucky: Bath, Haircut, House cleaning.

Avoid: Starting a construction, Moving to a new house, Wedding.

Weekly goals/ to do:

_____
_____
_____
_____

14 (09/19)   **Friday**
                                              Geng Zi (庚子) - Earth
Happiness star: **Northwest**, Wealth star: **East**
Conflicting sign: **Horse,** Conflicting direction: **South**

Lucky: Ceremony, Bath, Haircut, Setting up a bed, Starting a business, Training animals, Funeral.
Avoid: Wedding, Moving to a new house, Starting a construction, Activating Feng Shui cures.

15 (09/20)   Saturday
                                              Xin Chou (辛丑) - Earth
Happiness star: **Southwest**, Wealth star: **East**
Conflicting sign: **Goat,** Conflicting direction: **east**

Lucky: Ceremony, Fixing animal houses.
Avoid: Any major festive event.

16 (09/21)   Sunday
                                              Ren Yin (壬寅) - Metal
Happiness star: **South**, Wealth star: **South**
Conflicting sign: **Monkey,** Conflicting direction: **North**

Lucky: Funeral, Hunting.
Avoid: Any major festive event, Visiting sick patients.

Weekly review/ gratitude:

_____
_____
_____
_____

October 2022

Week 43

October

S	M	T	W	T	F	S
25	26	27	28	29	30	1
2	3	4	5	6	7	8
9	10	11	12	13	14	15
16	17	18	19	20	21	22
23	24	25	26	27	28	29
30	31	1	2	3	4	5

---

17 (lunar date: 09/22)   **Monday**

Kui Mao (癸卯) - Metal

Happiness star: **Southeast**, Wealth star: **South**
Conflicting sign: **Rooster,** Conflicting direction: **West**

Lucky: Ceremony, Activating Feng Shui cures, Travel, Dressmaking, Wedding, Starting a construction, Moving to a new house, Adopting animals, Planting, Funeral.
Avoid: None.

---

18 (09/23)   **Tuesday**

Jia Chen (甲辰) - Fire

Happiness star: **Northeast**, Wealth star: **Southeast**
Conflicting sign: **Dog,** Conflicting direction: **South**

Lucky: Ceremony, Removing Feng Shui cures, Bath, Demolition.
Avoid: Any major festive event.

---

19 (09/24)   **Wednesday**

Yi Si (乙巳) - Fire

Happiness star: **Northwest**, Wealth star: **Southeast**
Conflicting sign: **Pig,** Conflicting direction: **East**

Lucky: Ceremony, Signing a contract, Wedding, Dressmaking, Meeting friends, Setting up a bed, Hunting.
Avoid: Funeral, Sharp knives.

---

20 (09/25)   **Thursday**

Bing Wu (丙午) - Water

Happiness star: **Southwest**, Wealth star: **West**
Conflicting sign: **Rat,** Conflicting direction: **North**

Lucky: Ceremony, Travel, Starting a business, Funeral, Dressmaking, Setting up a bed, Visiting a doctor.
Avoid: Wedding, Moving to a new house, Setting up a stove, Sharp knives.

Weekly goals/ to do:
_____
_____
_____
_____

---

21 (09/26)   **Friday**
                                                     Ding Wei (丁未) - Water
Happiness star: **South**, Wealth star: **West**
Conflicting sign: **Ox** Conflicting direction: **West**

Lucky: Ceremony, Hunting.
Avoid: Starting a business, Setting up a door/stove, Wedding, Moving to a new house, Funeral.

---

22 (09/27)   Saturday
                                                     Wu Shen (戊申) - Earth
Happiness star: **Southeast**, Wealth star: **North**
Conflicting sign: **Tiger,** Conflicting direction: **South**

Lucky: Ceremony, Travel, Haircut, Meeting friends, Removing Feng Shui cures, Starting a business, House cleaning, Planting, Adopting animals, Visiting a doctor.
Avoid: Wedding, Moving to a new house, Funeral.

---

23 (09/28) ** Frost Descent (Shung Jiang 霜降)*   Sunday
                                                     Yi You (己酉) - Earth
Happiness star: **Northeast** Wealth star: **North**
Conflicting sign: **Rabbit,** Conflicting direction: **East**

Lucky: Ceremony, Bath, Removing Feng Shui cures, Haircut, Dressmaking, Setting up a bed/stove, House cleaning, Pest control, Fixing animal houses.
Avoid: Wedding, Moving to a new house, Funeral.

Weekly review/ gratitude:
_____
_____
_____
_____

October 2022

Week 44

October

S	M	T	W	T	F	S
25	26	27	28	29	30	1
2	3	4	5	6	7	8
9	10	11	12	13	14	15
16	17	18	19	20	21	22
23	24	25	26	27	28	29
30	31	1	2	3	4	5

---

24 (lunar date: 09/29)   **Monday**

Geng Xu (庚戌) - Metal

Happiness star: **Northwest,** Wealth star: **East**

Conflicting sign: **Dragon,** Conflicting direction: **North**

Lucky: Ceremony, Travel, Dressmaking, Wedding, Meeting friends, Training animals, Adopting animals, Moving to a new house.

Avoid: Start a construction, Funeral.

---

25 (10/01)   **Tuesday**

Xin Hai (辛亥) - Metal

Happiness star: **Southwest,** Wealth star: **East**

Conflicting sign: **Snake,** Conflicting direction: **West**

Lucky: Ceremony, Activating Feng Shui cures, Travel, Bath, Haircut, Meeting friends, Setting up a bed, Moving to a new house.

Avoid: Wedding, Signing a contract.

---

26 (10/02)   **Wednesday**

Ren Zi (壬子) - Wood

Happiness star: **South,** Wealth star: **South**

Conflicting sign: **Horse,** Conflicting direction: **South**

Lucky: Ceremony, Starting a business, Funeral, Bath, Haircut, Meeting friends, Trading, Training animals, Funeral.

Avoid: Wedding, Moving to a new house, Starting a construction.

---

27 (10/03)   **Thursday**

Kui Chou (癸丑) - Wood

Happiness star: **Southeast,** Wealth star: **South**

Conflicting sign: **Goat,** Conflicting direction: **East**

Lucky: Fixing a street/walkway, Fixing animal houses.

Avoid: Any major festive event.

28 (10/04)

Happiness star: **Northeast**, Wealth star: **Southeast**
Conflicting sign: **Monkey,** Conflicting direction: **North**

Friday
Jia Yin (甲寅) - Water

Lucky: Funeral, Hunting.
Avoid: Visiting sick patients, **Any major festive event.**

---

29 (10/05)

Happiness star: **Northwest**, Wealth star: **Southeast**
Conflicting sign: **Rooster,** Conflicting direction: **West**

Saturday
Yi Mao (乙卯) - Water

Lucky: Ceremony, Hunting, Fishing, Funeral.
Avoid: Visiting sick patients, Wedding, Moving to a new house.

---

30 (10/06)

Happiness star: **Southwest**, Wealth star: **West**
Conflicting sign: **Dog,** Conflicting direction: **South**

Sunday
Bing Chen (丙辰) - Earth

Lucky: Ceremony, Removing Feng Shui cures, Bath, Demolition.
Avoid: Any major festive event.

Weekly review/ gratitude:

October - November 2022

Week 45

November

S	M	T	W	T	F	S
30	31	1	2	3	4	5
6	7	8	9	10	11	12
13	14	15	16	17	18	19
20	21	22	23	24	25	26
27	28	29	30	1	2	3

---

31 (lunar date: 10/07)

Monday

Ding Si (丁巳) - Earth

Happiness star: **South**, Wealth star: **West**

Conflicting sign: **Pig**, Conflicting direction: **East**

Lucky: Ceremony, Signing a contract, Meeting friends, Hunting, Adopting animals.
Avoid: Moving to a new house, Activating Feng Shui cures, Funeral, Sharp knives.

Nov 1 (10/08)

Tuesday

Wu Wu (戊午) - Fire

Happiness star: **Southeast**, Wealth star: **North**

Conflicting sign: **Rat**, Conflicting direction: **North**

Lucky: Ceremony, Activate Feng Shui cures, Travel, Wedding, Dressmaking, Setting up a bed, Adopting animals.
Avoid: Starting a construction, Starting a business, Funeral, Sharp knives.

---

2 (10/09)

Wednesday

Ji Wei (己未) - Fire

Happiness star: **Northeast**, Wealth star: **North**

Conflicting sign: **Ox**, Conflicting direction: **West**

Lucky: Ceremony, Setting up a stove, Hunting, Pest control.
Avoid: Wedding, Setting up a door, Funeral.

---

3 (10/10)

Thursday

Geng Shen (庚申) - Wood

Happiness star: **Northwest**, Wealth star: **East**

Conflicting sign: **Tiger**, Conflicting direction: **South**

Lucky: Ceremony, Dressmaking, Setting up a stove, Starting a business, Planting.
Avoid: Moving to a new house, Activating Feng Shui cures, Setting up a bed.

Weekly goals/ to do:

---

4 (10/11)   **Friday**
Xin You (辛酉) - Wood

Happiness star: **Southwest**   Wealth star: **East**
Conflicting sign: **Rabbit,**   Conflicting direction: **East**

Lucky: Ceremony, Travel, Bath, Haircut, Dressmaking, Wedding, Setting up a bed/stove, Training animals, Planting, Funeral.
Avoid: Activating Feng Shui cures, Setting up a door, Starting a business.

---

5 (10/12)   **Saturday**
Ren Xu (壬戌) - Water

Happiness star: **South,**   Wealth star: **South**
Conflicting sign: **Dragon,**   Conflicting direction: **North**

Lucky: Ceremony, Activating Feng Shui cures, Travel, Signing a contract, Wedding, Setting up a bed/stove, Moving to a new house, Adopting animals, Visiting a doctor.
Avoid: Starting a construction, Funeral.

---

6 (10/13)   **Sunday**
Kui Hai (癸亥) - Water

Happiness star: **Southeast,**   Wealth star: **South**
Conflicting sign: **Snake,**   Conflicting direction: **West**

Lucky: Ceremony, Bath, Haircut, Dressmaking, House cleaning, Removing Feng Shui cures.
Avoid: Wedding,.

Weekly review/ gratitude:

November 2022

Week 46

November

S	M	T	W	T	F	S
30	31	1	2	3	4	5
6	7	8	9	10	11	12
13	14	15	16	17	18	19
20	21	22	23	24	25	26
27	28	29	30	1	2	3

---

7 (lunar date: 10/14) * *Start of Winter (Li Dong 立冬)*

Monday
Jia Zi (甲子) - Metal

Happiness star: **Northeast**, Wealth star: **Southeast**
Conflicting sign: **Horse**, Conflicting direction: **South**

Lucky: Ceremony, Bath, Haircut, Funeral, Visiting a doctor.
Avoid: Activating Feng Shui cures, Moving to a new house.

---

8 (10/15)

Tuesday
Yi Chou (乙丑) - Metal

Happiness star: **Northwest**, Wealth star: **Southeast**
Conflicting sign: **Goat,** Conflicting direction: **East**

Lucky: None.
Avoid: Any major festive event.

---

9 (10/16)

Wednesday
Bing Yin (丙寅) - Fire

Happiness star: **Southwest**, Wealth star: **West**
Conflicting sign: **Monkey,** Conflicting direction: **North**

Lucky: Travel, Dressmaking, Starting a construction, Setting up a bed, Starting a business, Funeral, Trading, Planting, Adopting animals.
Avoid: Wedding, Setting up a bed, Ceremony.

---

10 (10/17)

Thursday
Ding Mao (丁卯) - Fire

Happiness star: **South**, Wealth star: **West**
Conflicting sign: **Rooster,** Conflicting direction: **West**

Lucky: Ceremony, Travel, Starting a construction, Setting up a bed, Moving to a new house, Starting a business, Activating Feng Shui cures, Dressmaking.
Avoid: Wedding, Setting up a stove.

Weekly goals/ to do:

_____
_____
_____
_____

11 (10/18)   **Friday**
Happiness star: **Southeast,** Wealth star: **North**   Wu Chen (戊辰) - Wood
Conflicting sign: **Dog,** Conflicting direction: **South**

Lucky: Ceremony, Bath, Haircut, Dressmaking, Wedding, Meeting friends, Setting up a bed, Hunting, Funeral, Visiting a doctor.
Avoid: Activating Feng Shui cures, Starting a construction, Starting a business.

12 (10/19)   Saturday
Happiness star: **Northeast,** Wealth star: **North**   Ji Si (己巳) - Wood
Conflicting sign: **Pig,** Conflicting direction: **East**

Lucky: Ceremony, Removing Feng Shui cures, Visiting a doctor, Demolition.
Avoid: Any major festive event.

13 (10/20)   Sunday
Happiness star: **Northwest,** Wealth star: **East**   Geng Wu (庚午) - Earth
Conflicting sign: **Rat,** Conflicting direction: **North**

Lucky: Ceremony, Activating Feng Shui cures, Travel, Wedding, Starting a construction, Starting a business, Planting, Adopting animals, Funeral.
Avoid: Visiting sick patients.

Weekly review/ gratitude:

_____
_____
_____
_____

November 2022

Week 47

November

S	M	T	W	T	F	S
30	31	1	2	3	4	5
6	7	8	9	10	11	12
13	14	15	16	17	18	19
20	21	22	23	24	25	26
27	28	29	30	1	2	3

---

14 (lunar date: 10/21)　　　　　　　　　　　**Monday**
Xin Wei (辛未) - Earth

Happiness star: **Southwest**, Wealth star: **East**
Conflicting sign: **Ox,** Conflicting direction: **West**

Lucky: Ceremony, Starting a construction, Setting up a bed/stove, Trading, Planting, Adopting animals, Funeral, Activating Feng Shui cures.
Avoid: Wedding, Moving to a new house.

---

15 (10/22)　　　　　　　　　　　　　　　**Tuesday**
Ren Shen (壬申) - Metal

Happiness star: **South**, Wealth star: **South**
Conflicting sign: **Tiger,** Conflicting direction: **South**

Lucky: Ceremony, Bath, House cleaning, Hunting, Pest control.
Avoid: Any major festive event, Sharp knives.

---

16 (10/23)　　　　　　　　　　　　**Wednesday**
Kui You (癸酉) - Metal

Happiness star: **Southeast**, Wealth star: **South**
Conflicting sign: **Rabbit,** Conflicting direction: **East**

Lucky: Ceremony, Bath, Dressmaking, Starting a construction, Setting up a bed, Starting a business, Trading, Planting.
Avoid: Wedding, Moving to a new house, Activating Feng Shui cures, Funeral, Sharp knives.

---

17 (10/24)　　　　　　　　　　　　　**Thursday**
Jia Xu (甲戌) - Fire

Happiness star: **Northeast**, Wealth star: **Southeast**
Conflicting sign: **Dragon,** Conflicting direction: **North**

Lucky: Ceremony, Travel, Signing a contract, Wedding, Starting a construction, Pest control, Funeral.
Avoid: Moving to a new house.

Weekly goals/ to do:
_____
_____
_____
_____

---

18 (10/25)   **Friday**
Happiness star: **Northwest**, Wealth star: **Southeast**   Yi Hai (乙亥) - Fire
Conflicting sign: **Snake,** Conflicting direction: **West**

Lucky: Ceremony, Travel, Bath.
Avoid: Wedding, Moving to a new house, Starting a construction.

---

19 (10/26)   Saturday
Happiness star: **Southwest**, Wealth star: **West**   Bing Zi (丙子) - Water
Conflicting sign: **Horse,** Conflicting direction: **South**

Lucky: Travel, Wedding, Starting a construction, Starting a business, Planting, Adopting animals,
Funeral, Visiting a doctor.
Avoid: Setting up a bed/stove, Activating Feng Shui cures.

---

20 (10/27)   Sunday
Happiness star: **South**, Wealth star: **West**   Ding Chou (丁丑) - Water
Conflicting sign: **Goat,** Conflicting direction: **East**

Lucky: Ceremony, Pest control.
Avoid: Wedding, Moving to a new house, Starting a construction, Funeral, Setting up a stove.

Weekly review/ gratitude:
_____
_____
_____
_____

November 2022

Week 48

November

S	M	T	W	T	F	S
30	31	1	2	3	4	5
6	7	8	9	10	11	12
13	14	15	16	17	18	19
20	21	22	23	24	25	26
27	28	29	30	1	2	3

---

21 (lunar date: 10/28)

Monday
Wu Yin (戊寅) - Earth

Happiness star: **Southeast**, Wealth star: **North**
Conflicting sign: **Monkey**, Conflicting direction: **North**

Lucky: Travel, Activating Feng Shui cures, Dressmaking, Setting up a door, Moving to a new house, Starting a business, Adopting animals, Funeral.
Avoid: Wedding.

---

22 (10/29) ** Lesser Snow (Xiao Xue 小雪)*

Tuesday
Ji Mao (己卯) - Earth

Happiness star: **Northeast**, Wealth star: **North**
Conflicting sign: **Rooster**, Conflicting direction: **West**

Lucky: Ceremony, Travel, Wedding, Starting a construction, Setting up a stove, Moving to a new house, Planting, Funeral, Activating Feng Shui cures.
Avoid: Visiting sick patients.

---

23 (10/30)

Wednesday
Geng Chen (庚辰) - Metal

Happiness star: **Northwest**, Wealth star: **East**
Conflicting sign: **Dog**, Conflicting direction: **South**

Lucky: Ceremony, Travel, Wedding, Dressmaking, Setting up a door/bed, Moving to a new house, Planting, Adopting animals, Funeral.
Avoid: Starting a construction, Starting a business, Activating Feng Shui cures.

---

24 (11/01)

Thursday
Xin Si (辛巳) - Metal

Happiness star: **Southwest**, Wealth star: **East**
Conflicting sign: **Pig**, Conflicting direction: **East**

Lucky: Demolition, Visiting a doctor.
Avoid: Any major festive event.

25 (11/02)   **Friday**

Ren Wu (壬午) - Wood

Happiness star: **South**, Wealth star: **South**
Conflicting sign: **Rat,** Conflicting direction: **North**

Lucky: Ceremony, Activating Feng Shui cures, Travel, Wedding, Dressmaking, Hunting, Adopting animals.
Avoid: Visiting sick patients, Funeral.

26 (11/03)   Saturday

Kui Wei (癸未) - Wood

Happiness star: **Southeast**, Wealth star: **South**
Conflicting sign: **Ox,** Conflicting direction: **West**

Lucky: Ceremony, Bath, Removing Feng Shui cures, Meeting friends, Adopting animals, Planting, Funeral.
Avoid: Wedding, Moving to a new house, Starting a business, Starting a construction, Activating Feng Shui cures.

27 (11/04)   Sunday

Jia Shen (甲申) - Water

Happiness star: **Northeast**, Wealth star: **Southeast**
Conflicting sign: **Tiger,** Conflicting direction: **South**

Lucky: Ceremony, Haircut, House cleaning, Pest control.
Avoid: Any major festive event, Sharp knives.

Weekly review/ gratitude:

November - December 2022

Week 49

December

S	M	T	W	T	F	S
27	28	29	30	1	2	3
4	5	6	7	8	9	10
11	12	13	14	15	16	17
18	19	20	21	22	23	24
25	26	27	28	29	30	31

---

28 (lunar date: 11/05)

Happiness star: **Northwest**, Wealth star: **Southeast**
Conflicting sign: **Rabbit,** Conflicting direction: **East**

Monday
Yi You (乙酉) - Water

Lucky: Ceremony, Activating Feng Shui cures, Wedding, Starting a construction, Setting up a bed, Starting a business, Adopting animals, Dressmaking.
Avoid: Sharp knives, Moving to a new house, Funeral.

---

29 (11/06)

Happiness star: **Southwest**, Wealth star: **West**
Conflicting sign: **Dragon,** Conflicting direction: **North**

Tuesday
Bing Xu (丙戌) - Earth

Lucky: Ceremony, Dressmaking, Wedding, Setting up a bed, Pest control, Hunting.
Avoid: Funeral.

---

30 (11/07)

Happiness star: **South**, Wealth star: **West**
Conflicting sign: **Snake,** Conflicting direction: **West**

Wednesday
Ding Hai (丁亥) - Earth

Lucky: Ceremony, Bath.
Avoid: Starting a construction, Starting a business, Wedding, Moving to a new house, Funeral.

Dec 1 (11/08)

Happiness star: **Southeast**, Wealth star: **North**
Conflicting sign: **Horse,** Conflicting direction: **South**

Thursday
Wu Zi (戊子) - Fire

Lucky: Travel, Activating Feng Shui cures, Wedding, Starting a construction, Moving to a new house, Starting a business, Funeral, Visiting a doctor, Fixing animal houses.
Avoid: Setting up a bed.

Weekly goals/ to do:

_____

_____

_____

_____

2 (11/09)   **Friday**
                                              Ji Chou (己丑) - Fire
Happiness star: **Northeast**, Wealth star: **North**
Conflicting sign: **Goat,** Conflicting direction: **East**

Lucky: Ceremony, Bath, Haircut, Dressmaking, Meeting friends, Setting up a bed, Pest control.
Avoid: Wedding, Moving to a new house, Travel, Activating Feng Shui cures, Funeral.

3 (11/10)   Saturday
                                            Geng Yin (庚寅) - Wood
Happiness star: **Northwest**, Wealth star: **East**
Conflicting sign: **Monkey,** Conflicting direction: **North**

Lucky: Travel, Activating Feng Shui cures, Wedding, Start a construction, Setting up a bed,
Moving to a new house, Funeral.
Avoid: Starting a business.

4 (11/11)   Sunday
                                             Xin Mao (辛卯) - Wood
Happiness star: **Southwest**, Wealth star: **East**
Conflicting sign: **Rooster,** Conflicting direction: **West**

Lucky: Ceremony, Travel, Starting a construction, Setting up a stove, Moving to a new house,
Starting a business, Trading, Adopting animals, Funeral.
Avoid: Wedding, Activating Feng Shui cures.

Weekly review/ gratitude:

_____

_____

_____

_____

December 2022

Week 50

December

S	M	T	W	T	F	S
27	28	29	30	1	2	3
4	5	6	7	8	9	10
11	12	13	14	15	16	17
18	19	20	21	22	23	24
25	26	27	28	29	30	31

---

5 (lunar date: 11/12)   **Monday**

Ren Chen (壬辰) - Water

Happiness star: **South**, Wealth star: **South**

Conflicting sign: **Dog,** Conflicting direction: **South**

Lucky: Ceremony, Wedding, Bath, Haircut, Removing Feng Shui cures, Fishing, Hunting.

Avoid: Funeral, Starting a construction, Moving to a new house.

---

6 (11/13)   **Tuesday**

Kui Si (癸巳) - Water

Happiness star: **Southeast**, Wealth star: **South**

Conflicting sign: **Pig,** Conflicting direction: **East**

Lucky: Demolition, Visiting a doctor.

Avoid: Any major festive event.

---

7 (11/14) *Greater Snow (Da Xue 大雪)*   **Wednesday**

Jia Wu (甲午) - Metal

Happiness star: **Northeast**, Wealth star: **Southeast**

Conflicting sign: **Rat,** Conflicting direction: **North**

Lucky: Ceremony, Travel, Activating Feng Shui cures, Setting up a bed, Moving to a new house, Adopting animals, Funeral.

Avoid: Any major festive event.

---

8 (11/15)   **Thursday**

Yi Wei (乙未) - Metal

Happiness star: **Northwest**, Wealth star: **Southeast**

Conflicting sign: **Ox,** Conflicting direction: **West**

Lucky: Ceremony, Travel, Dressmaking, Setting up a bed, Hunting.

Avoid: Wedding, Starting a construction, Activating Feng Shui cures, Moving to a new house.

9 (11/16)

Happiness star: **Southwest**, Wealth star: **West**

Conflicting sign: **Tiger,** Conflicting direction: **South**

Friday
Bing Shen (丙申) - Fire

Lucky: Ceremony, Activating Feng Shui cures, Travel, Bath, Wedding, Moving to a new house, Hunting, Adopting animals, Funeral, Visiting a doctor.

Avoid: Starting a construction, Starting a business.

---

10 (11/17)

Happiness star: **South**, Wealth star: **West**

Conflicting sign: **Rabbit,** Conflicting direction: **East**

Saturday
Ding You (丁酉) - Fire

Lucky: Ceremony, Bath, Dressmaking, Setting up a bed, House cleaning, Pest control, Hunting, Planting.

Avoid: Sharp knives, Wedding, Starting a business, Activating Feng Shui cures, Funeral.

---

11 (11/18)

Happiness star: **Southeast,** Wealth star: **North**

Conflicting sign: **Dragon,** Conflicting direction: **North**

Sunday
Wu Xu (戊戌) - Wood

Lucky: Dressmaking, Activating Feng Shui cures, Signing a contract, Dressmaking, Meeting friends, Starting a construction, Planting, Adopting animals.

Avoid: Wedding, Moving to a new house, Starting a business, Funeral.

Weekly review/ gratitude:

December 2022

Week 51

December

S	M	T	W	T	F	S
27	28	29	30	1	2	3
4	5	6	7	8	9	10
11	12	13	14	15	16	17
18	19	20	21	22	23	24
25	26	27	28	29	30	31

---

12 (lunar date: 11/19)   **Monday**
                                                      Ji Hai (己亥) - Wood

Happiness star: **Northeast**, Wealth star: **North**

Conflicting sign: **Snake**, Conflicting direction: **West**

Lucky: Travel, Bath, Haircut, Starting a construction, Moving to a new house, Dressmaking, Setting up a door, Pest control.
Avoid: Wedding, Setting up a bed, Activating Feng Shui cures.

---

13 (11/20)   **Tuesday**
                                                    Geng Zi (庚子) - Earth

Happiness star: **Northwest**, Wealth star: **East**

Conflicting sign: **Horse**, Conflicting direction: **South**

Lucky: Training animals.
Avoid: Any major festive event.

---

14 (11/21)   **Wednesday**
                                                   Xin Chou (辛丑) - Earth

Happiness star: **Southwest**, Wealth star: **East**

Conflicting sign: **Goat**, Conflicting direction: **East**

Lucky: Ceremony, Travel, Dressmaking, Wedding, Meeting friends, Setting up a bed, Starting a construction, Starting a business, Trading, House cleaning, Planting, Adopting animals.
Avoid: Moving to a new house, Funeral.

---

15 (11/22)   **Thursday**
                                                     Ren Yin (壬寅) - Metal

Happiness star: **South**, Wealth star: **South**

Conflicting sign: **Monkey**, Conflicting direction: **North**

Lucky: Activating Feng Shui cures, Setting up a bed, Planting, Funeral, Visiting a doctor.
Avoid: Wedding, Starting a construction, Moving to a new house, Visiting sick patients.

Weekly goals/ to do:

---

16 (11/23)   **Friday**
                                                        Kui Mao (癸卯) - Metal
Happiness star: **Southeast**, Wealth star: **South**
Conflicting sign: **Rooster**, Conflicting direction: **West**

Lucky: Demolition, Fixing a street/walkway.
Avoid: Any major festive event.

---

17 (11/24)   Saturday
                                                        Jia Chen (甲辰) - Fire
Happiness star: **Northeast** Wealth star: **Southeast**
Conflicting sign: **Dog**, Conflicting direction: **South**

Lucky: Ceremony, Travel, Wedding, Starting a construction, Moving to a new house, Planting, Adopting animals, Funeral, Activating Feng Shui cures.
Avoid: Starting a business.

---

18 (11/25)   Sunday
                                                        Yi Si (乙巳) - Fire
Happiness star: **Northwest**, Wealth star: **Southwest**
Conflicting sign: **Pig**, Conflicting direction: **East**

Lucky: Ceremony, Bath, Dressmaking, Meeting friends, Starting a construction, Setting up a door/bed/stove.
Avoid: Wedding, Moving to a new house, Activating Feng Shui cures, Funeral, Starting a business,.

Weekly review/ gratitude:

December 2022

Week 52

December

S	M	T	W	T	F	S
27	28	29	30	1	2	3
4	5	6	7	8	9	10
11	12	13	14	15	16	17
18	19	20	21	22	23	24
25	26	27	28	29	30	31

---

19 (lunar date: 11/26)   **Monday**

Happiness star: **Southwest**, Wealth star: **West**   Bing Wu (丙午) - Fire

Conflicting sign: **Rat,** Conflicting direction: **North**

Lucky: Ceremony, Demolition, Visiting a doctor.

Avoid: Any major festive event.

---

20 (11/27)   **Tuesday**

Happiness star: **South**, Wealth star: **West**   Ding Wei (丁未) - Water

Conflicting sign: **Ox,** Conflicting direction: **West**

Lucky: Ceremony, Travel, Starting a construction, Setting up a bed, Starting a business, Trading, Hunting, Funeral.

Avoid: Wedding, Moving to a new house, Activating Feng Shui cures.

---

21 (11/28)   **Wednesday**

Happiness star: **Southeast**, Wealth star: **North**   Wu Shen (戊申) - Earth

Conflicting sign: **Tiger,** Conflicting direction: **South**

Lucky: Ceremony, Activating Feng Shui cures, Dressmaking, Adopting animals, Funeral, Visiting a doctor.

Avoid: Wedding, Setting up a bed, Starting a construction, Sharp knives.

---

22 (11/29) * *Winter Solstice (Dong Zhi 冬至)*   **Thursday**

Happiness star: **Northeast**, Wealth star: **North**   Ji You (己酉) - Earth

Conflicting sign: **Rabbit,** Conflicting direction: **East**

Lucky: Ceremony, Bath, Haircut, House cleaning, Hunting, Planting.

Avoid: Sharp knives, Wedding, Moving to a new house, Funeral.

Weekly goals/ to do:

---

23 (12/01)   **Friday**

Happiness star: **Northwest**, Wealth star: **East**   Geng Xu (庚戌) - Metal

Conflicting sign: **Dragon,** Conflicting direction: **North**

Lucky: Ceremony, Adopting animals, Activating Feng Shui cures, Dressmaking, Starting a construction, Setting up a bed/door, Planting.

Avoid: Wedding, Moving to a new house, Funeral.

---

24 (12/02)   **Saturday**

Happiness star: **Southwest**, Wealth star: **East**   Xin Hai (辛亥) - Metal

Conflicting sign: **Snake,** Conflicting direction: **West**

Lucky: Ceremony, Dressmaking, Bath, Starting a construction, Setting up a door/stove, Pest control, Planting.

Avoid: Activating Feng Shui cures, Setting up a bed, Wedding.

---

25 (12/03)   Sunday

Happiness star: **South**, Wealth star: **South**   Ren Zi (壬子) - Wood

Conflicting sign: **Horse,** Conflicting direction: **South**

Lucky: Funeral.

Avoid: Wedding, Moving to a new house, Starting a construction.

Weekly review/ gratitude:

December 2022 - January 2023

Week 53

December

S	M	T	W	T	F	S
27	28	29	30	1	2	3
4	5	6	7	8	9	10
11	12	13	14	15	16	17
18	19	20	21	22	23	24
25	26	27	28	29	30	31

---

26 (lunar date: 12/04)   **Monday**
                                                                Kui Chou (癸丑) - Wood

Happiness star: **Southeast,** Wealth star: **South**

Conflicting sign: **Goat,** Conflicting direction: **East**

Lucky: Ceremony, Bath, Dressmaking, Starting a construction, Starting a business, Planting, Adopting animals.

Avoid: Wedding, Moving to a new house, Activating Feng Shui cures, Funeral.

---

27 (12/05)   **Tuesday**
                                                                  Jia Yin (甲寅) - Water

Happiness star: **Northeast,** Wealth star: **Southeast**

Conflicting sign: **Monkey,** Conflicting direction: **North**

Lucky: Activating Feng Shui cures, Dressmaking, Setting up a door/bed, Trading, Funeral, Visiting a doctor.

Avoid: Wedding, Moving to a new house, Starting a construction, Visiting sick patients.

---

28 (12/06)   **Wednesday**
                                                                  Yi Mao (乙卯) - Water

Happiness star: **Northwest,** Wealth star: **Southeast**

Conflicting sign: **Rooster,** Conflicting direction: **West**

Lucky: Ceremony, Fixing a street/walkway.

Avoid: Any major festive event, Visiting sick patients.

---

29 (12/07)   **Thursday**
                                                                Bing Chen (丙辰) - Earth

Happiness star: **Southwest,** Wealth star: **West**

Conflicting sign: **Dog,** Conflicting direction: **South**

Lucky: Ceremony, Starting a construction, Setting up a door, Moving to a new house, Adopting animals, Funeral, Travel.

Avoid: Wedding, Activating Feng Shui cures, Setting up a bed/stove, Starting a business.

Weekly goals/ to do:

_____
_____
_____
_____

30 (12/08)   **Friday**
Happiness star: **South,** Wealth star: **West**   Ding Si (丁巳) - Earth
Conflicting sign: **Pig,** Conflicting direction: **East**

Lucky: Ceremony, Hunting, Fishing, Pest control.
Avoid: Any major festive event.

31 (12/09)   Saturday
Happiness star: **Southwest,** Wealth star: **North**   Wu Wu (戊午) - Fire
Conflicting sign: **Rat,** Conflicting direction: **North**

Lucky: Ceremony, Bath, Demolition.
Avoid: Any major festive event.

Jan 1, 2023 (12/10)   Sunday
Happiness star: **Northeast,** Wealth star: **North**   Ji Wei (己未) - Fire
Conflicting sign: **Ox,** Conflicting direction: **West**

Lucky: Ceremony, Starting a construction, Setting up a bed, Hunting, Fishing.
Avoid: Activating Feng Shui cures, Setting up a door/stove, Wedding, Funeral.

Weekly review/ gratitude:

_____
_____
_____
_____

January 2023

Week 1

January

S	M	T	W	T	F	S
1	2	3	4	5	6	7
8	9	10	11	12	13	14
15	16	17	18	19	20	21
22	23	24	25	26	27	28
29	30	31	1	2	3	4

---

2 (lunar date: 12/11)   **Monday**

Happiness star: **Northwest**, Wealth star: **East**   Geng Shen (庚申) - Wood

Conflicting sign: **Tiger**, Conflicting direction: **South**

Lucky: Ceremony, Activating Feng Shui cures, Travel, Wedding, Funeral, Setting up a stove, Visiting a doctor.

Avoid: Starting a construction, Starting a business, Moving to a new house, Sharp knives.

---

3 (12/12)   **Tuesday**

Happiness star: **Southwest**, Wealth star: **East**   Xin You (辛酉) - Wood

Conflicting sign: **Rabbit**, Conflicting direction: **East**

Lucky: Ceremony, Activating Feng Shui cures, Dressmaking, Setting up a bed/stove, Bath, Haircut, Training animals, Fishing, Hunting, Pest control.

Avoid: Starting a construction, Wedding, Moving to a new house, Funeral, Sharp knives.

---

4 (12/13)   **Wednesday**

Happiness star: **South**, Wealth star: **South**   Ren Xu (壬戌) - Water

Conflicting sign: **Dragon**, Conflicting direction: **North**

Lucky: Ceremony, Activating Feng Shui cures, Dressmaking, Meeting friends, Starting a construction, Setting up a door/bed/stove, Starting a business, Adopting animals, Planting.

Avoid: Wedding, Moving to a new house, Funeral.

---

5 (12/14) * *Lesser Cold (Xiao Han 小寒)*   **Thursday**

Happiness star: **Southeast**, Wealth star: **South**   Hui Hai (癸亥) - Water

Conflicting sign: **Snake**, Conflicting direction: **West**

Lucky: Bath, Haircut, Visiting a doctor, Meeting friends, Setting up a stove, Fixing animal houses, Starting a construction.

Avoid: Wedding, Setting up a bed, Moving to a new house, Activating Feng Shui cures, Funeral.

Weekly goals/ to do:

---

6 (12/15)
Happiness star: **Northeast**, Wealth star: **Southeast**
Conflicting sign: **Horse,** Conflicting direction: **South**

Friday
Jia Zi (甲子) - Metal

Lucky: Ceremony, Dressmaking, Setting up a door/bed/stove, Adopting animals, Funeral.
Avoid: Wedding, Moving to a new house, Activating Feng Shui cures, Starting a construction.

---

7 (12/16)
Happiness star: **Northwest** Wealth star: **Southwest**
Conflicting sign: **Goat,** Conflicting direction: **East**

Saturday
Yi Chou (乙丑) - Metal

Lucky: Ceremony, Removing Feng Shui cures, Meeting friends.
Avoid: Any major festive event.

---

8 (12/17)
Happiness star: **Southwest**, Wealth star: **West**
Conflicting sign: **Monkey,** Conflicting direction: **North**

Sunday
Bing Yin (丙寅) - Fire

Lucky: Activating Feng Shui cures, Dressmaking, Starting a construction, Setting up a bed,
Moving to a new house, Trading, Starting a business, Visiting a doctor.
Avoid: Wedding, Funeral.

Weekly review/ gratitude:

January 2023

Week 2

January

S	M	T	W	T	F	S
1	2	3	4	5	6	7
8	9	10	11	12	13	14
15	16	17	18	19	20	21
22	23	24	25	26	27	28
29	30	31	1	2	3	4

---

9 (lunar date: 12/18)   **Monday**
Ding Mao (丁卯) - Fire

Happiness star: **South**, Wealth star: **West**
Conflicting sign: **Rooster**, Conflicting direction: **West**

Lucky: Ceremony, Travel, Signing a contract, Dressmaking, Wedding, Meeting friends, Setting up a bed, Starting a business, Trading, Planting, Funeral.
Avoid: Activating Feng Shui cures, Moving to a new house, Starting a construction.

---

10 (12/19)   **Tuesday**
Wu Chen (戊辰) - Wood

Happiness star: **Southeast**, Wealth star: **North**
Conflicting sign: **Dog,** Conflicting direction: **South**

Lucky: Ceremony, Fixing a street/walkway.
Avoid: Any major festive event.

---

11 (12/20)   **Wednesday**
Ji Si (己巳) - Wood

Happiness star: **Northeast**, Wealth star: **North**
Conflicting sign: **Pig,** Conflicting direction: **East**

Lucky: Ceremony, Activating Feng Shui cures, Wedding, Meeting friends, Starting a construction, Setting up a bed/stove, Moving to a new house, Adopting animals, Dressmaking.
Avoid: Starting a business, Funeral.

---

12 (12/21)   **Thursday**
Geng Wu (庚午) - Earth

Happiness star: **Northwest**, Wealth star: **East**
Conflicting sign: **Rat,** Conflicting direction: **North**

Lucky: Ceremony, Travel, Wedding, Starting a construction, Setting up a bed, Planting, Adopting animals, Funeral, Activating Feng Shui cures.
Avoid: Visiting sick patients, Setting up a door, Moving to a new house.

Weekly goals/ to do:

_____
_____
_____
_____

---

13 (12/22)   **Friday**
                                                              Xin Wei (辛未) - Earth
Happiness star: **Southwest**, Wealth star: **East**
Conflicting sign: **Ox,** Conflicting direction: **West**

Lucky: Ceremony, Removing Feng Shui cures, Demolition.
Avoid: Any major festive event.

---

14 (12/23)   Saturday
                                                              Ren Shen (壬申) - Metal
Happiness star: **South,** Wealth star: **South**
Conflicting sign: **Tiger,** Conflicting direction: **South**

Lucky: Ceremony, Starting a construction, Starting a business, Trading, Hunting, Planting,
Adopting animals, Funeral.
Avoid: Activating Feng Shui cures, Moving to a new house, Wedding, Sharp knives.

---

15 (12/24)   Sunday
                                                              Kui You (癸酉) - Metal
Happiness star: **Southeast**, Wealth star: **South**
Conflicting sign: **Rabbit,** Conflicting direction: **East**

Lucky: Ceremony, Bath, Haircut, House cleaning, Funeral.
Avoid: Any major festive event, Sharp knives.

Weekly review/ gratitude:

_____
_____
_____
_____

January 2023

Week 3

January

S	M	T	W	T	F	S
1	2	3	4	5	6	7
8	9	10	11	12	13	14
15	16	17	18	19	20	21
22	23	24	25	26	27	28
29	30	31	1	2	3	4

---

16 (lunar date: 12/25)   **Monday**
Jia Xu (甲戌) - Fire

Happiness star: **Northeast**, Wealth star: **Southeast**
Conflicting sign: **Dragon**, Conflicting direction: **North**

Lucky: Ceremony, Activating Feng Shui cures, Setting up a stove, Hunting, Planting, Pest control.
Avoid: Wedding, Moving to a new house, Starting a business, Setting up a bed, Funeral.

---

17 (12/26)   **Tuesday**
Yi Hai (乙亥) - Fire

Happiness star: **Northwest**, Wealth star: **Southeast**
Conflicting sign: **Snake**, Conflicting direction: **West**

Lucky: Ceremony, Dressmaking, Setting up a bed/stove, Moving to a new house, Starting a business, Trading, Adopting animals, Visiting a doctor.
Avoid: Activating Feng Shui cures, Wedding.

---

18 (12/27)   **Wednesday**
Bing Zi (丙子) - Water

Happiness star: **Southwest**, Wealth star: **West**
Conflicting sign: **Horse**, Conflicting direction: **South**

Lucky: Ceremony, Bath, Dressmaking, Setting up a bed, Trading, Funeral.
Avoid: Wedding, Moving to a new house, Starting a construction, Starting a business.

---

19 (12/28)   **Thursday**
Ding Chou (丁丑) - Water

Happiness star: **South**, Wealth star: **West**
Conflicting sign: **Goat**, Conflicting direction: **East**

Lucky: Ceremony, Removing Feng Shui cures, Training animals.
Avoid: Any major festive event.

---

20 (12/29) * *Greater Cold (Da Han 大寒)*   **Friday**
                                                    Wu Yin (戊寅) - Earth
Happiness star: **Southeast**, Wealth star: **North**
Conflicting sign: **Monkey** Conflicting direction: **North**

Lucky: Dressmaking, Wedding, Setting up a bed, Moving to a new house, Starting a business, Trading, Funeral, Activating Feng Shui cures.
Avoid: Adopting animals.

---

21 (12/30)   Saturday
                                                    Ji Mao (己卯) - Earth
Happiness star: **Northeast**, Wealth star: **North**
Conflicting sign: **Rooster,** Conflicting direction: **West**

Lucky: Ceremony, Dressmaking, Wedding, Meeting friends, Setting up a bed, Trading, Adopting animals.
Avoid: Visiting sick patients, Moving to a new house, Funeral.

---

22 (01/01/2023) * *Lunar New Year (Rabbit Year)*   Sunday
                                                    Geng Chen (庚辰) - Metal
Happiness star: **Northwest**, Wealth star: **East**
Conflicting sign: **Dog,** Conflicting direction: **South**

Lucky: Ceremony, Dressmaking, Setting up a bed, Fixing a street/walkway, Funeral.
Avoid: Wedding, Funeral.

Weekly review/ gratitude:

January 2023

Week 4

January

S	M	T	W	T	F	S
1	2	3	4	5	6	7
8	9	10	11	12	13	14
15	16	17	18	19	20	21
22	23	24	25	26	27	28
29	30	31	1	2	3	4

---

23 (lunar date: 01/02)   **Monday**
                                                       Xin Si (辛巳) - Metal

Happiness star: **Southwest**, Wealth star: **East**

Conflicting sign: **Pig,** Conflicting direction: **East**

Lucky: Ceremony, Signing a contract, Wedding, Meeting friends, Adopting animals.

Avoid: Moving to a new house, Starting a business, Funeral.

---

24 (01/03)   **Tuesday**
                                                       Ren Wu (壬午) - Wood

Happiness star: **South**, Wealth star: **South**

Conflicting sign: **Rat,** Conflicting direction: **North**

Lucky: Ceremony, Travel, Bath, Dressmaking, Wedding, Setting up a bed, Moving to a new house, Hunting, Funeral.

Avoid: Visiting sick patients, Activating Feng Shui cures, Setting up a door, Starting a construction.

---

25 (01/04)   **Wednesday**
                                                       Kui Wei (癸未) - Wood

Happiness star: **Southeast**, Wealth star: **South**

Conflicting sign: **Ox,** Conflicting direction: **West**

Lucky: Ceremony, Demolition.

Avoid: Any major festive event.

---

26 (01/05)   **Thursday**
                                                       Jia Shen (甲申) - Water

Happiness star: **Northeast**, Wealth star: **Southeast**

Conflicting sign: **Tiger,** Conflicting direction: **South**

Lucky: Ceremony, Activating Feng Shui cures, Wedding, Dressmaking, Setting up a stove, Moving to a new house, Starting a business, Planting, Adopting animals, Funeral.

Avoid: Starting a construction, Sharp knives.

Weekly goals/ to do:

_____

_____

_____

_____

27 (01/06)

Friday
Yi You (乙酉) - Water

Happiness star: **Northwest**, Wealth star: **Southeast**

Conflicting sign: **Rabbit,** Conflicting direction: **East**

Lucky: Ceremony, House cleaning, Funeral.

Avoid: Sharp knives, **Any major festive event.**

28 (01/07)

Saturday
Bing Xu (丙戌) - Earth

Happiness star: **Southwest**, Wealth star: **West**

Conflicting sign: **Dragon ,** Conflicting direction: **North**

Lucky: Ceremony, Hunting, Pest control, Fishing.

Avoid: Wedding, Moving to a new house, Starting a business, Setting up a bed, Funeral.

29 (01/08)

Sunday
Ding Hai (丁亥) - Earth

Happiness star: **South**, Wealth star: **West**

Conflicting sign: **Snake,** Conflicting direction: **West**

Lucky: Ceremony, Travel, Activating Feng Shui cures, Dressmaking, Setting up a bed, Moving to a new house, Starting a business, Trading, Visiting a doctor.

Avoid: Wedding, Setting up a stove.

Weekly review/ gratitude:

_____

_____

_____

_____

January - February 2023

Week 5

February

S	M	T	W	T	F	S
29	30	31	1	2	3	4
5	6	7	8	9	10	11
12	13	14	15	16	17	18
19	20	21	22	23	24	25
26	27	28	1	2	3	4

---

30 (lunar date: 01/09)   **Monday**
                                                        Wu Zi (戊子) - Fire

Happiness star: **Southeast**, Wealth star: **North**

Conflicting sign: **Horse**, Conflicting direction: **South**

Lucky: Ceremony, Bath, Dressmaking, Setting up a bed, Trading, Funeral.

Avoid: Wedding, Moving to a new house, Starting a construction, Activating Feng Shui cures.

---

31 (01/10)   **Tuesday**
                                                       Yi Chou (己丑) - Fire

Happiness star: **Northeast**, Wealth star: **North**

Conflicting sign: **Goat,** Conflicting direction: **East**

Lucky: Ceremony, Removing Feng Shui cures, Training animals, Fixing animal houses.

Avoid: Any major festive event.

Feb 1, 2023 (01/11)   **Wednesday**
                                                      Geng Yin (庚寅) - Wood

Happiness star: **Northwest**, Wealth star: **East**

Conflicting sign: **Monkey,** Conflicting direction: **North**

Lucky: Travel, Bath, Haircut, Signing a contract, Wedding, Starting a business, Planting, Adopting animals, Funeral, Visiting a doctor.

Avoid: Activating Feng Shui cures, Moving to a new house, Starting a construction.

---

2 (01/12)   **Thursday**
                                                       Xin Mao (辛卯) - Wood

Happiness star: **Southwest**, Wealth star: **East**

Conflicting sign: **Rooster,** Conflicting direction: **West**

Lucky: Travel, Ceremony, Activating Feng Shui cures, Dressmaking, Wedding, Setting up a bed, Starting a business, Funeral.

Avoid: Moving to a new house, Starting a construction.

Weekly goals/ to do:

_____

_____

_____

_____

---

3 (01/13)   **Friday**

Ren Chen (壬辰) - Water

Happiness star: **South,** Wealth star: **South**

Conflicting sign: **Dog,** Conflicting direction: **South**

Lucky: Fixing a street/walkway.

Avoid: Any major festive event.

---

4 (01/14) ** Start of Spring (Li Chun 立春)*   Saturday

Kui Si (癸巳) - Water

Happiness star: **Southeast,** Wealth star: **South**

Conflicting sign: **Pig,** Conflicting direction: **East**

Lucky: Ceremony, Activating Feng Shui cures, Dressmaking, Setting up a stove, Moving to a new house, Adopting animals.

Avoid: Wedding, Funeral.

---

5 (01/15) ** Lantern Festival*   Sunday

Jia Wu (甲午) - Metal

Happiness star: **Northeast,** Wealth star: **Southeast**

Conflicting sign: **Rat,** Conflicting direction: **North**

Lucky: Ceremony, Travel, Dressmaking, Starting a construction, Setting up a bed, Moving to a new house, Starting a business, Adopting animals, Building animal houses.

Avoid: Wedding. Funeral.

Weekly review/ gratitude:

_____

_____

_____

_____

February 2023

Week 6

February

S	M	T	W	T	F	S
29	30	31	1	2	3	4
5	6	7	8	9	10	11
12	13	14	15	16	17	18
19	20	21	22	23	24	25
26	27	28	1	2	3	4

---

6 (lunar date: 01/16)   **Monday**
Happiness star: **Northwest,** Wealth star: **Southeast**   Yi Wei (乙未) - Metal
Conflicting sign: **Ox,** Conflicting direction: **West**

Lucky: Ceremony, Dressmaking, Wedding, Setting up a door/bed, Moving to a new house, Fishing, Hunting, Funeral.
Avoid: None.

---

7 (01/17)   **Tuesday**
Happiness star: **Southwest,** Wealth star: **West**   Bing Shen (丙申) - Fire
Conflicting sign: **Tiger,** Conflicting direction: **South**

Lucky: Demolition, Visiting a doctor, Bath, Removing Feng Shui cures.
Avoid: Any major festive event.

---

8 (01/18)   **Wednesday**
Happiness star: **South,** Wealth star: **West**   Ding You (丁酉) - Fire
Conflicting sign: **Rabbit,** Conflicting direction: **East**

Lucky: Ceremony, Travel, Wedding, Starting a construction, Moving to a new house, Adopting animals, Funeral.
Avoid: Setting up a bed.

---

9 (01/19)   **Thursday**
Happiness star: **Southeast** Wealth star: **North**   Wu Xu (戊戌) - Wood
Conflicting sign: **Dragon,** Conflicting direction: **North**

Lucky: Pest control, Fishing, Hunting, Funeral.
Avoid: Any major festive event.

10 (01/20)

Friday
Ji Hai (己亥) - Wood

Happiness star: **Northeast**, Wealth star: **North**
Conflicting sign: **Snake**, Conflicting direction: **West**

Lucky: Ceremony, Bath, Haircut, Signing a contract, Dressmaking, Setting up a bed, Fishing, Planting.
Avoid: Wedding, Moving to a new house, Funeral.

11 (01/21)

Saturday
Geng Zi (庚子) - Earth

Happiness star: **Northwest**, Wealth star: **East**
Conflicting sign: **Horse**, Conflicting direction: **South**

Lucky: Ceremony, Travel, Bath, Haircut, Wedding.
Avoid: Setting up a bed, Moving to a new house, Funeral, Sharp knives, Starting a construction.

12 (01/22)

Sunday
Xin Chou (辛丑) - Earth

Happiness star: **Southwest**, Wealth star: **East**
Conflicting sign: **Goat,** Conflicting direction: **East**

Lucky: Ceremony, Funeral.
Avoid: Wedding, Moving to a new house, Setting up a door, Starting a construction.

Weekly review/ gratitude:

February 2023

Week 7

February

S	M	T	W	T	F	S
29	30	31	1	2	3	4
5	6	7	8	9	10	11
12	13	14	15	16	17	18
19	20	21	22	23	24	25
26	27	28	1	2	3	4

---

13 (lunar date: 01/23)

Monday
Ren Yin (壬寅) - Metal

Happiness star: **South,** Wealth star: **South**

Conflicting sign: **Monkey,** Conflicting direction: **North**

Lucky: Dressmaking, Meeting friends, Setting up a bed, Trading, Adopting animals, Funeral.
Avoid: Wedding, Moving to a new house, Travel, Activating Feng Shui cures,Visiting sick patients.

---

14 (01/24)

Tuesday
Kui Mao (癸卯) - Metal

Happiness star: **Southeast,** Wealth star: **South**

Conflicting sign: **Rooster,** Conflicting direction: **West**

Lucky: Ceremony, Activating Feng Shui cures, Travel, Wedding, Starting a construction, Setting up a bed, Moving to a new house, Starting a business, Adopting animals, Funeral.
Avoid: Visiting a doctor.

---

15 (01/25)

Wednesday
Jia Chen (甲辰) - Fire

Happiness star: **Northeast,** Wealth star: **Southeast**

Conflicting sign: **Dog,** Conflicting direction: **South**

Lucky: Ceremony, Dressmaking, Meeting friends, Setting up a bed.
Avoid: Wedding, Moving to a new house, Funeral, Starting a business, Setting up a door.

---

16 (01/26)

Thursday
Yi Si (乙巳) - Fire

Happiness star: **Northwest,** Wealth star: **Southeast**

Conflicting sign: **Pig,** Conflicting direction: **East**

Lucky: Setting up a stove, Fixing a street/walkway.
Avoid: Wedding, Moving to a new house, Funeral.

_____
_____
_____
_____

17 (01/27)   **Friday**
                                              Bing Wu (丙午) - Water
Happiness star: **Southwest**, Wealth star: **West**
Conflicting sign: **Rat**, Conflicting direction: **North**

Lucky: Ceremony, Travel, Wedding, Starting a construction, Setting up a bed, Moving to a new house, Starting a business, Planting, Adopting animals, Funeral.
Avoid: Activating Feng Shui cures.

18 (01/28)   Saturday
                                             Ding Wei (丁未) - Water
Happiness star: **South**, Wealth star: **West**
Conflicting sign: **Ox**, Conflicting direction: **West**

Lucky: Ceremony, Travel, Dressmaking, Wedding, Starting a construction, Setting up a bed, Moving to a new house, Planting, Adopting animals, Funeral.
Avoid: None.

19 (01/29) * _Rain Water (Yu Shui 雨水)_   Sunday
                                             Wu Shen (戊申) - Earth
Happiness star: **Southeast**, Wealth star: **North**
Conflicting sign: **Tiger**, Conflicting direction: **South**

Lucky: Ceremony, Removing Feng Shui cures, Bath, Visiting a doctor, Demolition, House cleaning.
Avoid: Any major festive event.

Weekly review/ gratitude:

_____
_____
_____
_____

February 2023

Week 8

February

S	M	T	W	T	F	S
29	30	31	1	2	3	4
5	6	7	8	9	10	11
12	13	14	15	16	17	18
19	20	21	22	23	24	25
26	27	28	1	2	3	4

---

20 (lunar date: 02/01)

Monday
Ji You (己酉) - Earth

Happiness star: **Northeast**, Wealth star: **North**
Conflicting sign: **Rabbit**, Conflicting direction: **East**

Lucky: Ceremony, Activating Feng Shui cures, Travel, Dressmaking, Starting a construction, Moving to a new house, Starting a business, Funeral.
Avoid: Wedding, Setting up a bed.

---

21 (02/02)

Tuesday
Geng Xu (庚戌) - Metal

Happiness star: **Northwest**, Wealth star: **East**
Conflicting sign: **Dragon**, Conflicting direction: **North**

Lucky: Funeral, Pest control.
Avoid: Any major festive event.

---

22 (02/03)

Wednesday
Xin Hai (辛亥) - Metal

Happiness star: **Southwest**, Wealth star: **East**
Conflicting sign: **Snake**, Conflicting direction: **West**

Lucky: Ceremony, Activating Feng Shui cures, Starting a construction, Setting up a bed/stove, Moving to a new house, Training animals, Planting, Adopting animals.
Avoid: Wedding, Starting a business, Funeral, Sharp knives.

---

23 (02/04)

Thursday
Ren Zi (壬子) - Wood

Happiness star: **South**, Wealth star: **South**
Conflicting sign: **Horse** Conflicting direction: **South**

Lucky: Ceremony, Activating Feng Shui cures, Haircut, Wedding, Starting a construction, Planting, Visiting a doctor.
Avoid: Moving to a new house, Starting a business, Funeral, Sharp knives.

---

24 (02/05)   **Friday**

Happiness star: **Southeast**, Wealth star: **South**   Kui Chou (癸丑) - Wood

Conflicting sign: **Goat** Conflicting direction: **East**

Lucky: Ceremony, Dressmaking, Setting up a bed/stove, Funeral.

Avoid: Wedding, Moving to a new house, Starting a construction.

---

25 (02/06)   **Saturday**

Happiness star: **Northeast**, Wealth star: **Southeast**   Jia Yin (甲寅) - Water

Conflicting sign: **Monkey,** Conflicting direction: **North**

Lucky: Dressmaking, Meeting friends, Starting a business, Trading, Training animals, Adopting animals.

Avoid: Wedding, Moving to a new house, Activating Feng Shui cures, Funeral, Visiting sick patients.

---

26 (02/07)   **Sunday**

Happiness star: **Northwest**, Wealth star: **Southeast**   Yi Mao (乙卯) - Water

Conflicting sign: **Rooster,** Conflicting direction: **West**

Lucky: Ceremony, Travel, Starting a construction, Setting up a bed, Moving to a new house, Starting a business, Trading, Funeral, Visiting a doctor.

Avoid: Wedding, Activating Feng Shui cures.

Weekly review/ gratitude:

February 2023

Week 9

March

S	M	T	W	T	F	S
26	27	28	1	2	3	4
5	6	7	8	9	10	11
12	13	14	15	16	17	18
19	20	21	22	23	24	25
26	27	28	29	30	31	1

---

27 (lunar date: 02/08)   **Monday**
Bing Chen (丙辰) - Earth

Happiness star: **Southwest**, Wealth star: **West**
Conflicting sign: **Dog,** Conflicting direction: **South**

Lucky: Ceremony, Activating Feng Shui cures, Travel, Dressmaking, Wedding, Meeting friends, Setting up a bed, Moving to a new house, Adopting animals.
Avoid: Starting a construction, Starting a business, Funeral, Setting up a stove.

---

28 (02/09)   **Tuesday**
Ding Si (丁巳) - Earth

Happiness star: **South**, Wealth star: **West**
Conflicting sign: **Pig,** Conflicting direction: **East**

Lucky: Ceremony, Fixing a street/walkway.
Avoid: Wedding, Funeral, Travel.

Mar 1, 2023 (02/10)   **Wednesday**
Wu Wu (戊午) - Fire

Happiness star: **Southeast**, Wealth star: **North**
Conflicting sign: **Rat,** Conflicting direction: **North**

Lucky: Signing a contract, Ceremony, Travel, Starting a business, Moving to a new house, Trading, Setting up a door/bed, Funeral.
Avoid: Activating Feng Shui cures, Starting a construction, Setting up a stove.

---

2 (02/11)   **Thursday**
Ji Wei (己未) - Fire

Happiness star: **Northeast**, Wealth star: **North**
Conflicting sign: **Ox,** Conflicting direction: **West**

Lucky: Starting a construction, Wedding, Funeral.
Avoid: Starting a business, Setting up a stove/bed, Moving to a new house, Dressmaking.

Weekly goals/ to do:

---

3 (02/12)

Happiness star: **Northwest**, Wealth star: **East**
Conflicting sign: **Tiger**, Conflicting direction: **South**

Friday
Geng Shen (庚申) - Wood

Lucky: Demolition, Visiting a doctor.
Avoid: Any major festive event.

---

4 (02/13)

Happiness star: **Southwest**, Wealth star: **East**
Conflicting sign: **Rabbit**, Conflicting direction: **East**

Saturday
Xin You (辛酉) - Wood

Lucky: Ceremony, Bath, Funeral.
Avoid: Starting a business, Wedding, Setting up a bed, Moving to a new house, Setting up a stove.

---

5 (02/14)

Happiness star: **South**, Wealth star: **South**
Conflicting sign: **Dragon**, Conflicting direction: **North**

Sunday
Ren Xu (壬戌) - Water

Lucky: Ceremony, Pest control, Fishing, Funeral.
Avoid: Wedding, Moving to a new house.

Weekly review/ gratitude:

My Career Planning
Long term goals

2022

2023

2024

2025

2026

2027

2028

2029

2030

2031

2032

2033

2022 monthly career goals

January

February

March

April

May

June

July

August

September

October

November

December

My Finance Planning
Long term goals

2022

2023

2024

2025

2026

2027

2028

2029

2030

2031

2032

2033

2022 monthly financial goals

January

February

March

April

May

June

July

August

September

October

November

December

My Health Planning
Long term goals

2022

2023

2024

2025

2026

2027

2028

2029

2030

2031

2032

2033

2022 monthly health goals

January

February

March

April

May

June

July

August

September

October

November

December

My Family/Relationships Planning
Long term goals

2022

2023

2024

2025

2026

2027

2028

2029

2030

2031

2032

2033

2022 monthly family goals

January

February

March

April

May

June

July

August

September

October

November

December

My Spiritual Planning
Long term goals

2022

2023

2024

2025

2026

2027

2028

2029

2030

2031

2032

2033

2022 monthly spiritual goals

January

February

March

April

May

June

July

August

September

October

November

December

My Hobby Planning
Long term goals

2022

2023

2024

2025

2026

2027

2028

2029

2030

2031

2032

2033

2022 monthly hobby goals

January

February

March

April

May

June

July

August

September

October

November

December

Notes

Printed in Great Britain
by Amazon

75500678R00115